SPANISH
GRAMMAR
FOR
BEGINNERS

A Comprehensive Workbook
with Essential Lessons
and Everyday Phrases

¡hola!

LINGO DISCOVERY

CONTENIDO

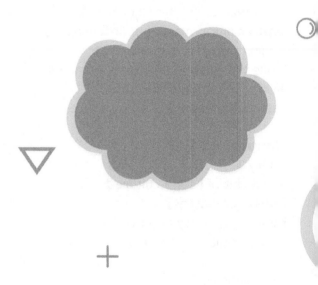

Introduction

*"One language sets you in a corridor for life.
Two languages open every door along the way."
-Frank Smith*

Learning a new language can be described as exciting, frightening, difficult, or enjoyable- maybe a mix of all of those. If learning languages were easy, then everyone would speak more than one. However, if you push through the more difficult concepts and keep practicing, you'll be proud of the progress you have made along the way.

This book will get you reading, writing, and speaking Spanish. It's very practical, with lots of exercises that get you actively engaging with the language. There are answers to the exercises at the back of the book, where you can check your progress should you want to. The book is varied in style, with word searches, fill-in-the-blanks, and connect-lines exercises, which help make learning fun. The lessons covered are practical in nature, and whether you're visiting Spain for a vacation, an exchange program, a business trip, or for some other reason, the vocab and phrases you learn here are bound to come in useful.

What this book covers

This book is designed especially for English speakers beginning to learn Spanish. It covers pronunciation, vocabulary, and grammar. You'll be able to improve your speaking, reading, and writing of Spanish by completing the lessons here. Some topics covered include: how to conjugate verbs in the past, present, and future, how to put together vocabulary to make flowing sentences, and how to understand written passages even when you don't know every word.

Study tips

Often, people study by staring at words and hoping their brains will soak them in. Perro means "dog", perro means "dog", perro means "dog". Unfortunately, staring at the words on the page is passive learning which is not as effective as active learning.

Active learning, by contrast, requires you to do something to practice the words. This type of learning is more effective. So here is a list of tips that may be useful for learning Spanish:

✔ **Be all ears!** If you have the chance, listen carefully in any Spanish-speaking experience you have. Feel free to ask questions as many times as you need if there is something you do not understand. In the beginning, you probably won't be able to understand everything, but even if you do not realize it, you are learning a lot!

✔ **Open your mouth!** Practice, practice, and practice speaking this new language every day. Speaking aloud gives you confidence, makes you identify your mistakes and speak better the next time. You may even sing! We have included a list of catchy tunes so you can sing aloud and experiment. Learning should be fun!

✔ **Get the picture!** Visualize the new vocabulary, see the pictures, and associate them with the Spanish words. Examples of active learning include making flashcards (yes, making flashcards is helpful, so consider making some by hand rather than by computer). You may also write the words you want to remember. For example, if you are learning new vocabulary related to the house, you can put signs with the names of the objects around your own house.

✔ **Put into practice!** Practicing daily is more effective than a long weekly practice session. Consistency and persistence are the clues to success.

✔ **Leave no stone unturned!** Explore everywhere! Put yourself in a Spanish context. Try to find some TV shows, newspapers, magazines, books, movies, webpages, or a Spanish-speaking friend or neighbor that may increase your contact with the language. This will make your learning easier and more effective.

✔ **Cross the bridge!** Help you connect all your experiences... related to immersing yourself in Spanish, will make you connect with many areas of your life, increase your comprehension and enrich your learning.

How to use this book

This book is divided into chapters that can each be completed in a day. However, there is no rush. Take the time you need.

Some chapters have a lot of vocabulary, so It will be helpful to review those words daily.

Happy learning!

CHAPTER 1

PRONUNCIATION

Do you know the difference between *esta* and *está* ("this" and "it is")? It's a tiny little line over the a. You will want to learn this important accent so you pronounce words correctly.

Spanish pronunciation vs. English pronunciation

English is a tough language. Just look at the words r*ough, bough, cough,* and *dough* and pronounce them all correctly. Imagine if you didn't just *know* how those words are pronounced, and you tried to learn them as a new language learner.

As a bilingual individual who has taught English and Spanish to non-native speakers, I believe Spanish pronunciation is easier to learn than English. It is common in English for a letter to stand for different sounds depending on the context and for the same sound to be represented by different letters. In contrast, once you know each letter's sound in Spanish (hint, the vowels and most consonants don't change sounds based on the situation like they do in English), then you can pronounce any new word you read in Spanish. This also helps you when you hear a word, because you will be able to know how it is spelled as soon as you hear it. This will help you be able to search for the word's pronunciation or write it down for later.

Example: *Esta* and *está.* The one without the mark over the letter a means "this", and the one with the mark over the letter a (á) means "it is". It also changes where you put the sound's force or stress. This may sound tricky, but let's get into this accent mark more specifically below.

The trick is that when you learn each Spanish sound, you can pronounce every word, so even though the new sounds may seem like a lot at the beginning, know that once you can remember the sounds, it will get much easier.

The Spanish diacritical marks

Before we get into each letter and its sound, let's go over a couple of marks you will see in Spanish words that you won't see in English ones.

In Spanish, we see three marked letters to indicate different pronunciations. They aren't just there for decoration, so as you learn to speak Spanish, make sure you pronounce them correctly.

Tilde

The first mark is called a tilde. It looks just like an accent mark, and hovers over the five vowels we are supposed to emphasize. It is written from lower left to upper right and is also used to distinguish words spelled similarly but with different meanings or usages.

Without tilde	a	e	i	o	u
With tilde	á	É	í	ó	ú

For example, *esta* and *está* are pronounced differently. The first sounds more like ES-tuh, and the second sounds like es-TAH. Whenever you see this accent mark, know that you have to emphasize that syllable or put more force into it when you say it.

To avoid learning rules on what syllables should be stressed when there is no accent mark or a tilde above a syllable, for now you can gradually learn how to pronounce them by paying attention to the pronunciation guide included after each new word in the vocabulary sections. Stressed syllables are underlined, bold or capitalized in the pronunciation guide.

Practice pronouncing these words and pay close attention to where the accent mark is located.

Papa (PA-pa) This means potato
Papá (pa-PA) This means father
Rápido (RAH- pee-dough) This means fast
Jamás (ha-MAS) This means never

Virgulilla

Another common mark you may see over the letter n in Spanish is this one: ~. It is called virgulilla (beer–goo–lee–yah.) Ñ is considered a different letter from *n*. However, because its pronunciation is so different, it's important to emphasize it now.

The *ñ* sounds more like a nyuh sound than an n sound. For example, *baño* is pronounced BAH-nyo.

Like with the tilde, the word's meaning can change if you don't focus on your pronunciation. Let's look at *moño* and *mono*. If you don't pay careful attention to Spanish pronunciation rules, you might pronounce these two words the same. This mistake isn't as grave as others, but it would be silly.

- *Moño* (MO-nyo) means "bun" as in a hair bun (not the type you eat).
- *Mono* (MO-no) means "monkey".

If you're trying to talk about your hair, you probably wouldn't be mentioning un mono!

Here is another pair of words that have changed meaning if you don't correctly pronounce ñ.

- *Ordeñar* (or-deh-NYAR) means "to milk something."
- *Ordenar* (or-deh-NAR) means "to put things in order."

You may see why this would be confusing. Pay careful attention to any type of mark over the letters in Spanish words and focus on your pronunciation. It might take more time initially, but you will feel more comfortable after some practice.

Diéresis - Spanish also uses a less common written umlaut above the letter u (ü) named - diéresis (dee-eh-reh-sihs). It is pronounced after the letter g in güe and güi, changing the sound "gu" into a "w".

The Spanish alphabet

Below is the Spanish alphabet and beside each letter you will find its pronunciation. The pronunciation has been written in two ways. The first form is according to the international phonetic alphabet. The second one is according to how it sounds as an English reader.

If you're already familiar with the phonetic alphabet, it may be easier to figure it out. However, the second pronunciation is also provided if you're ready to learn Spanish without knowing the phonetic alphabet.

Letter	Phonetic Pronunciation	English Pronunciation	Example
A	a	aaahh	Imagine you're at the dentist and need to open your mouth wide. Apagar (ah-pah-GAHR) (to turn off)
B	b	b	The *b* in Spanish is soft, like a mix between a b and a v sound. Ballena (bah-YEH-nah) (whale)
C	k	K or s	*Ca, Co*, and *cu* have a *k* sound like *ka, ko, koo*. Café (kah-FEH) (coffee), costa (KOHS-tah) (coast), cuchara (koo-CHAH-rah) (spoon). *Ce, ci* have an *s* sound like *seh, see* Cepillo (seh-PEE-yoh) (brush), cine (SEE-neh) (cinema)
D	d	duh	This sound is very similar to English. Dairy, Dino. Día (DEE-ah) (day)
E	e	eh	This sound is like the ones in elephant and elegant. Elefante (eh-leh-FAHN-teh) and elegante (eh-leh-GAHN-teh)
F	f	f	Very similar to English as well. Focus, fantastic, famous Foca (FOH-kah) (seal)

G	Y	heh	*Ga, go, gu.* It sounds like the g in gain before a, o and u. Gato (GAH-toh) (cat), gorila (goh-REE-lah) (gorilla), gusano(goo-SAH-noh) (worm) *Ge, gi.* It sounds like an English h as heaven and hill. Gente(HEHN-teh) (people), gigante (hee-GAHN-teh) (giant)
	X	H	*Gue, gui.* The vowel *u* is silent, and the letter *g* sounds like in the word *guest and guitar*. Guerra(GEH-rrah) (war), guisante(gee-SAHN-teh) (pea) Güe, güi. If the vowel *u* has a diaeresis, it's no longer silent. Desagüe (deh-SAH-gweh) (drain), *pingüino (peen-GWEE-noh) (penguin)*
H	No sound	silent	The *h* is silent in Spanish. Draw a line through it when you read *h* words if you need a visual reminder not to say anything. Hola (OH-lah) (hello)
I	i	ee	It sounds like the name of the letter 'e' in English. See, east, eagle inglés is pronounced (een-GLES)
J	H	huh	*J* sounds approximately like an *H* in English, but you should pronounce it at the back part of your tongue. *Jamón (ham)* is pronounced (ha-MON)
K	k	k	*K* is not often used in Spanish. Example words *kiwi, karate*

L	L	L	L is a little lighter in Spanish. Your tongue shouldn't touch your teeth. *León (leh-OHN) (lion).*
	y	Y	Double L has a y sound. *Llama (lama)* is pronounced YA-ma. *Llueve (it rains)* is pronounced YOU-eh-veh.
M	M	M	This sound is the same as in English. Try pronouncing these words- *mono (MOH-noh) (monkey), mamá (mah-MAH) (mother)*
N	N	N	Same sound as in English. Try these words- *nada (NAH-dah) (nothing), nadar(NAH-dhar) (to swim).*
Ñ	ñ	ny	This one is tricky (as we know from above). Try to pronounce it like an *n* and *y* sound together. *Moño (MOH-nyoh) (bun), niño (NEE-nyoh) (child)*
O	o	o	This letter sounds like a long *o* as the second o in octopus. *Ojo (eye)* (remember that *j* sounds like *h*). *Ojo* sounds like OH-ho
P	p	p	Same sound as in English. *Pan (pahn) (bread), punto (POON-toh) (point), pollo (chicken)* (pronounced POH-yoh)
Q	q	q	This letter sounds like a *k*. It always goes in combination with u, which is silent. *Queso (KEH-soh) (cheese).*

R	*r*	r	Very similar to the English sound. You only should roll your r if you see double *rr*. For example, *caro* means "expensive" and it is pronounced CA-ro. *Carro* means "car" and is pronounced the same but with a rolling *r* in the middle. At the beginning of the words, or after *l, n*, or *s*, it's always pronounced as a rolling r, although it's always written as a single r. For example *rosa (ROH-sah) (pink/rose), Enrique (Henry).*
	r	**rr**	
S	**s**	**s**	This is the same as English. *Solo (SOH-loh) (alone), salsa (SAHL-sah) (sauce), santo (SAHN- toh) (saint),* etc.
T	**t**	**t**	Also, the same English sound. *Tomate (toh-MAH-teh) (tomato)*
U	**w**	**ooh**	This is pronounced like ooooh. You've just seen something amazing, and you make the double oo sound like in food or goose. *Uvas (grapes)* is pronounced OO-bahs
V	**β**	**v**	The *v* is very soft in Spanish, a mix between the *b* and *v* sounds. Try saying vaso (BAH-soh) (glass)
W	**w**	**w**	Very similar to English. *Sándwich* is an example word, but there aren't many words that use this letter.
X	**ks**	**h**	In most words it is pronounced as *k* combined with *s*. For example *taxi, México* pronounced MEHK-he-co and *Texas* pronounced TEHK-shas.

Y	I	y	This letter is pronounced the same as in English. Example words would be *Ayer (yesterday)* pronounced ah-YAIR
Z	z	z	The *z* sound is softer than in English, more like an *s* than the vibrating z we think of in Spanish. *Zapato (shoe)* is pronounced with a soft z. sah-PAH-to

Note: Although it's not considered a separate letter, the blend *ch* is a common sound in Spanish. It sounds exactly like the ch sound in English words such as *China* or *church.* For example *ocho (oh-choh) (eight), techo (the-choh) (roof/ceiling).*

Pronunciation practice

Now that you have all the letter sounds, let's practice pronouncing them in words. Below are a few words to put the sounds into practice, starting with the easier ones and moving to the harder sounds. Try to read them through first without looking at the pronunciation. You can hide the pronunciation column. Remember that the stressed syllables in words without accent marks have been marked in bold for you!

SPANISH WORD	PRONUNCIATION	ENGLISH MEANING
Be**bé**	beh-beh	Baby
Mano	mah-no	Hand
Médico	me-dee-koh	Doctor
Libro	lee-bro	Book
Hola	oh-lah	Hello
Org**á**nico	ohr-gah-ni-ko	Organic
Plástico	plahs-tee-koh	Plastic
In**sec**to	een-sehk-toh	Insect
Ja**bón**	hah-bohn	Soap
Ja**món**	ha-moan	Ham
Niño	nee-nyo	Boy
Ara**ña**	ah-rah-nyah	Spider
Mon**ta**ña	Mohn-tah-nyah	Mountain

Lápiz	lah-pees	Pencil
Que**brar**	keh-brar	To break
Parque	pahr-keh	Park
Lluvia	yoo-byah	Rain
Calle	kah-yeh	Street
Choco**late**	Choh-koh-lah-teh	Chocolate
Barro	ba-rro	Mud

Tips for improving your pronunciation

Don't feel embarrassed as you attempt to pronounce new words. The more you try, The more comfortable you'll feel speaking. Here's a tip to help improve your pronunciation.

Find a song you like and see if there is a cover for it in Spanish or just search for reggaeton in Spanish, and you'll find some catchy music. Slow the speed of the video down so you can catch the words and just start repeating them. The more you say things aloud, the more the sounds, syllables, and words feel natural.

Here are a few songs that are fun to learn and sing out loud:

- "HASTA EL AMANECER" by Nicky Jam
- "ANDAS EN MI CABEZA" by Chino y Nacho
- "BAILA CONMIGO" by Selena Gomez
- "NO CREO" by Shakira
- "MACARENA" by Los del Río
- "GUANTANAMERA" by Celia Cruz
- "MATADOR" by Los Fabulosos Cadillacs
- "ERES TÚ" by Mocedades
- "LA MAZA" by Silvio Rodriguez
- "NO ME DOY POR VENCIDO" by Luis Fonsi
- "LA BAMBA" by Ritchie Valens
- "DANZA KUDURO" by Don Omar
- "COLGANDO EN TUS MANOS" by Carlos Baute
- "VIVIR MI VIDA" by Marc Anthony
- "BENDITA TU LUZ" by Maná
- "WAKA, WAKA" by Shakira
- "BURBUJA DE AMOR" by Juan Luis Guerra
- "AMIGO" by Roberto Carlos
- "SOMOS NOVIOS" by Armando Manzanero
- "BAILANDO" by Enrique Iglesias
- "TAN SOLO TÚ" by Franco De Vita
- "EL DÍA QUE ME QUIERAS" by Luis Miguel
- "ES POR TI" by Juanes

After you have had a chance to improve your pronunciation (even if you don't understand every word you are singing), go on to Chapter 2 to learn some vocabulary. If you would like a few more words to practice, read the words below out loud.

SPANISH WORD	PRONUNCIATION	ENGLISH MEANING
Mu**jer**	moo-hehr	Woman
Hijo	ee-hoh	Son
Esta**ción**	ehs-tah-syohn	Season/Station
Cu**chi**llo	koo-chee-yoh	Knife
Cua**der**no	kwah-dehr-noh	Notebook
Coci**ne**ro	koh-see-neh-roh	Cook
Es**pal**da	ehs-pahl-dah	Back
Pollo	poh-yoh	Chicken
Ga**lli**na	gah-yee-nah	Hen
Cer**ve**za	sehr-beh-sah	Beer
Ga**ra**je	gah-rah-heh	Garage
Al**muer**zo	ahl-mwehr-soh	Lunch
Fram**bue**sa	Frahm-bweh-sah	Raspberry
Mante**qui**lla	mahn-the-kee-yah	Butter
Dulce	dool-she	Sweet/Candy
Ramo	rrah-moh	Bouquet
Se**guir**	seh-geer	To follow
Ci**güe**ña	see-gweh-nyah	Stork
Alrede**dor**	ahl-rreh-deh-dohr	Around
Arqui**tec**to	ahr-kee-tehk-toh	Architect

CHAPTER 2

WELCOME

Greetings and Basics for Daily Life

Maybe you are learning Spanish because you are planning a trip or have a Spanish-speaking friend or need to know it for business purposes. Knowing the basics is a good idea to start with. Are you ready?

There are two ways of greeting a person in Spanish: formal and informal. You also have to pay attention to gender in some cases.

¡Hola!	Hello!
¡Buenos días!	Good morning!
¡Buenas tardes!	Good afternoon!
¡Buenas noches!	Good night!
¡Hasta pronto!	See you soon!
¡Hasta luego!	See you later!
¡Hasta mañana!	See you tomorrow!
Tengo que irme	I have to go
¡Nos vemos!	See you!
¡Adiós!	Goodbye!

LET'S PRACTICE!

Connect with lines.

Hello! •	• ¡Buenas noches!
Good morning! •	• ¡Buenos días!
Good afternoon! •	• ¡Hasta pronto!
Good night! •	• Tengo que irme
See you soon! •	• ¡Adiós!
See you later! •	• ¡Nos vemos!
See you tomorrow! •	• ¡Buenas tardes!
I have to go •	• ¡Hasta mañana!
See you! •	• ¡Hola!
Goodbye! •	• ¡Hasta luego!

Asking and responding how someone is...

¿Cómo estás? (informal)	How are you?
¿Cómo está? (formal)	How are you?
Mucho gusto	It is nice to meet you
Encantado/a	Nice to meet you
Bienvenido/a	Welcome
Estoy bien.	I am fine
Estoy muy cansado/a	I am very tired
No estoy bien	I am not OK
Estoy enfermo/a	I am sick
Estoy feliz	I am happy

LET'S PRACTICE!

How are you?	¿Cómo estás? (informal)
How are you?	(formal)
	Mucho gusto
Nice to meet you	
	Bienvenido/a
I am fine	
	Estoy muy cansado/a
I am not OK	
	Estoy enfermo/a
I am happy	

Introducing yourself

¿Cómo te llamas? (informal)	What is your name?
¿Cómo se llama? (formal)	What is your name?
¿De dónde eres? (informal)	Where are you from?
¿De dónde es usted? (formal)	Where are you from?
Me llamo	My name is
Mi nombre es	My name is
Soy de	I am from
Vivo en	I live in
¡Que tengas un buen día!	Have a good day!

How do we say.....in Spanish?

I am from	
Where are you from?	
My name is	
What is your name?	
I live in	
Have a good day!	
What is your name?	
What is your name?	

There is a cliché to start any conversation in any language. We will set some examples and you may practice with a friend as often as you want. In Spanish, we say **Buenos días** from 6 am to 12 pm (before having lunch), **Buenas tardes** after lunch until 8 pm (more or less) and **Buenas noches** after 9 pm.

- ¡Hola! ¡Buenos días!
- ¡Buenos días! ¿Cómo estás?
- Estoy bien. ¡Muchas gracias!
- ¡Adiós!
- ¡Hasta mañana!

- ¡Buenas tardes!
- ¡Buenas tardes! ¿Cómo te llamas?
- Me llamo Pedro. ¿Y tú? (and you?)
- Me llamo Juan
- ¡Mucho gusto!

- ¡Buenas noches!
- ¡Buenas noches! ¡Bienvenido! ¿Cómo estás?
- Estoy muy bien. ¡Muchas gracias! Soy Juan (I am Juan)
- ¡Hola, Juan! Me llamo Pedro.
- ¡Mucho gusto Pedro! ¿De dónde eres?
- Soy de España. ¿Y tú?
- Soy de Colombia.

It is time to create yours:

- ¡Buenos......................!
- ¡Buenos................! ¿Cómo.....................?
- Estoy.................................¡.............................! Soy ....
- ¡Bienvenida!
- ¡Encantada! ¿...?
- .... ¿...?
- Vivo en...
- ¡Que tengas un buen día!
- ¡Adiós!

Polite words

¡Muchas gracias!	Thank you very much"
Por favor	Please
¡De nada!	You are welcome!
¡Cuídate!	Take care!
Lo siento	I am sorry
Disculpas	I am sorry
Con permiso	Excuse me

LET'S PRACTICE!

Let's practice! Finding the correct words.

Find the Spanish words for:

1 Excuse me   **2** Take care   **3** I am sorry   **4** Hello

5 You are welcome   **6** I am sorry   **7** Thank you very much   **8** Please

9 My name is   **10** Nice to meet you   **11** I live in   **12** See you soon

13 Goodbye

Asking for help

¿Me puedes ayudar? (informal)	Can you help me?
¿Me puede ayudar? (formal)	Can you help me?
Necesito ayuda	I need help

Asking for directions

Disculpas, ¿dónde hay un supermercado?	Excuse me, where is a supermarket?
¿Hay un hospital por aquí?	Is there a hospital near here?
A la izquierda	To the left
A la derecha	To the right
Atrás	Behind
Cerca	Near
Lejos	Far
En frente	In front

LET'S PRACTICE!

Let´s practice! Connect with lines.

Is there a pharmacy near here? •	• Disculpas, ¿dónde está la biblioteca?
Can you help me? (formal) •	• ¿Hay una farmacia por aquí?
To the right •	• A la izquierda
Far •	• A la derecha
Can you help me? (informal) •	• Atrás
To the left •	• Cerca
Behind •	• Lejos
In front •	• En frente
Near •	• ¿Me puedes ayudar? (informal)
I need help •	• Necesito ayuda
Excuse me, where is the library? •	• ¿Me puede ayudar? (formal)

Colors

White	Yellow	Orange	Pink
Blanco	Amarillo	Naranja	Rosa

Red	Green	Light blue	Blue
Rojo	Verde	Celeste	Azul

Purple	Brown	Grey	Black
Morado	Marrón	Gris	Negro

Let's practice! Say it in Spanish!

1. Una mandarina es ………………………………… (a tangerine is……..)
2. Un plátano es ………………………………………….(a banana is …………)
3. Un delfín es ………………………………………… (a dolphin is……)
4. La luna es ……………………………………………..(the moon is ………….)
5. Un limón es …………………………………………..(a lemon is ……..)
6. El cielo es …………………………………………….(the sky is …………)
7. La planta es …………………………………………(the plant is …………..)
8. Los colores del semáforo son ……………………………………,
…………………………….. y ………………………… (the colors of the traffic lights
are……., ………., and …….)

Days of the week

Monday	lunes	loo-nehs
Tuesday	martes	mahr-tehs
Wednesday	miércoles	myehr-koh-lehs
Thursday	jueves	hweh-behs
Friday	viernes	byehr-nehs
Saturday	sábado	sah-bah-doh
Sunday	domingo	doh-meeng-goh

Months of the year

January	enero	eh-neh-roh
February	febrero	feh-breh-roh
March	marzo	mahr-soh
April	abril	ah-breel
May	mayo	mah-yoh
June	junio	hoo-nyoh
July	julio	hoo-lyoh
August	agosto	ah-gohs-toh
September	septiembre	sehp-tyehm-breh
October	octubre	ohk-too-breh
November	noviembre	noh-byehm-breh
December	diciembre	dee-syehm-breh

LET'S PRACTICE!

Complete each series:

1. Lunes, ………………….., miércoles, ………………………, viernes
2. Septiembre, ………………………., noviembre, ………………………… enero
3. Sábado, ……………….., ………………………., ………………………………
4. Marzo, …………………….., ………………………… junio, ………………………

Numbers

1	Uno	(oo-noh)	22	Veintidós	(beyn-tee-dohs)
2	Dos	(dohs)	23	Veintitrés	(beyn-tee-trehs)
3	Tres	(trehs)	24	Veinticuatro	(beyn-tee-kwah-troh)
4	Cuatro	(kwah-troh)	25	Veinticinco	(beyn-tee-seeng-koh)
5	Cinco	(seeng-koh)	26	Veintiséis	(beyn-tee-seys)
6	Seis	(seys)	27	Veintisiete	(beyn-tee-syeh-teh)
7	Siete	(syeh-teh)	28	Veintiocho	(beyn-tee-oh-choh)
8	Ocho	(oh-choh)	29	Veintinueve	(beyn-tee-nweh-beh)
9	Nueve	(nweh-beh)	30	Treinta	(treyn-tah)
10	Diez	(dyehs)	40	Cuarenta	(kwah-rehn-tah)
11	Once	(ohn-seh)	50	Cincuenta	(seeng-kwehn-tah)
12	Doce	(doh-seh)	60	Sesenta	(seh-sehn-tah)
13	Trece	(treh-seh)	70	Setenta	(seh-tehn-tah)
14	Catorce	(kah-tohr-seh)	80	Ochenta	(oh-chehn-tah)
15	Quince	(keen-seh)	90	Noventa	(noh-behn-tah)
16	Dieciséis	(dyeh-see-seys)	100	Cien	(syehn)
17	Diecisiete	(dyeh-see-syeh-teh)	500	Quinientos	(kee-nyehn-tohs)
18	Dieciocho	(dyeh-see-oh-choh)	1000	Mil	(meel)
19	Diecinueve	(dyeh-see-nweh-beh)	5000	Cinco mil	(seeng-koh-meel)
20	Veinte	(beyn-teh)	10000	Diez mil	(dyehs-meel)
21	Veintiuno	(beyn-tyoo-noh)	20000	Veinte mil	(beyn-teh-meel)

LET´S PRACTICE!

Say the numbers in Spanish!

1. Months of the year:
2. Days of the week:
3. Hours in a day:
4. Sides in two triangles:
5. Fingers on one hand:
6. Fingers on two hands:
7. Fingers on three hands:
8. Fingers on ten hands:
9. Insect legs:
10. Sides in one square:
11. Sides in two squares:
12. Your cell phone number:

CHAPTER 3

SUBJECT PRONOUNS, FEMININE AND MASCULINE, ARTICLES, AND COMMON NOUNS

Before learning about the subject pronouns used in Spanish, here is a quick refresher on a subject pronoun in English. Pronouns are short words that stand in place of people's names. For example, instead of saying Bob or Annie, you would use "he" or "she" The basic pronouns in English are *I, you, he, she, we, you and they.*

One difference between the pronouns used in English and Spanish is the word "you". In English, "you" can be used as a plural or singular pronoun. Depending on what part of the English-speaking world you are from, you might use phrases such as ya'll or you guys when talking about groups. Spanish has a separate pronoun for 'a group of you,' and you will learn that as the pronouns are introduced.

Another main difference between English and Spanish that you must get used to is that in Spanish you don't need to always use subject pronouns. But we'll return to this later.

Here is the basic chart. Memorize this list as it's not long and will help you understand sentences when we get to that point.

Personal pronoun		When do we use it
Yo	I	It refers to me
Tú	You	It refers to the person you are talking to in an informal way
Usted	You	It refers to the person you are talking to in a formal way
Él	He	It refers to a boy or a man
Ella	She	It refers to a girl or a woman
Nosotros	We	It refers a group of people including me
Nosotras	We (fem)	It refers a group of people including me (for girls or women)
Vosotros	You	It refers to you and you in Spain (not in Latin America)
Vosotras	You (fem)	It refers to you and you in Spain only women
Ellos	They	It refers to he and he or he and she
Ellas	They (fem)	It refers to she and she (girls or women)
Ustedes	You	It refers a group of people without you included

This list looks a little longer than the English list because there is a formal and informal you in Spanish.

"Tú" would be how you would address people you are close to, your children, or other family members.

"Usted" is for people you don't know well or would be used when you want to show respect.

When we talk about verbs later, we will focus on how the verbs are different depending on which type of 'you' you use.

LET´S PRACTICE!

Read these sentences aloud and figure out whom they are talking about based on the list of pronouns above. You may connect them with lines.

Yo voy a la tienda. •	• She is my friend.
Ellos estudian todos los días. •	• We are going to Costa Rica.
Nosotros vamos a Costa Rica. •	• I am going to the store.
Ella es mi amiga. •	• They study every day.

These pronouns are often used, so knowing them will give you a good basis for the rest of the language.

You may recognize -el to mean "the" (check back on the section called "El and La.") How can it also mean he? Well, there is one difference between the two words. Look at them side by side.
- el - the
- él- he

One has the tilde you learned about in the first chapter. The other one doesn't. While it doesn't change the pronunciation in this case, it *does* make it easier to differentiate when writing or reading Spanish. When you hear Spanish, look at the context around the word to figure out which meaning it is taking on for that sentence.

Feminine and masculine

In the English language, there are very few feminine and masculine nouns. There are some examples, such as *waitress* and *waiter, actress* and *actor*, but not many. Most of our nouns are just that- nouns- people, places, and things.

However, in Spanish, every noun is considered masculine or feminine. It is called its gender. So, it is important to understand whether feminine or masculine will impact the article and the adjectives that come around that noun. This is the case with many languages besides English.

How to recognize masculine and feminine genders?

If you are new to learning Spanish, it can be difficult to determine if something is masculine or feminine. If you're talking about a person, that's easy. But a table? Is a table a male or a female? Let me give you a hint since looking under the table won't help you. However, the last letter of every word *will*.

The easiest and most common rule is that a noun ending with *a* will be feminine and a noun ending with *o* will be masculine. That's ALMOST always true. For example,

Feminine	Masculine
mesa (table)	libro (book)
silla (chair)	disco (disc)
planta (plant)	equipo (team)
manzana (apple)	producto (product)
pelota (ball)	zapato (shoe)
muñeca (doll)	beso (kiss)
vida (life)	río (river)
respuesta (answer)	edificio (building)
carta (letter)	cuchillo (knife)
escuela (school)	pueblo (town)

There are exceptions, but you just have to memorize them as you come across them. Also, if a noun is masculine or feminine, like *libro* above, it is always masculine or feminine. The *mesa* won't be masculine in one sentence and feminine in the next one. Mesa is always feminine.

The exception is if a noun is a person or some animals. If it is male, then the noun is masculine, and vice versa. Please, look at the list below and see that all these feminine nouns end with *a* and use *una* in front of them and all these masculine nouns finish with o and we use *un* before it. *Una* and un mean a in Spanish, if the noun is feminine or masculine.

Feminine	English word	Masculine
Una niña	A girl/boy	Un niño
Una mesera	A waitress/waiter	Un mesero
Una gata	A cat	Un gato
Una perra	A dog	Un perro
Una maestra	A teacher	Un maestro
Una jugadora	A player	Un jugador
Una arquitecta	An arquitect	Un arquitecto
Una osa	A bear	Un oso
Una amiga	A friend	Un amigo
Una propietaria	An owner	Un propietario

Can you notice the difference when you would use *una* and *un*? In the next section, we will get into definitive articles (the). But for now, just remember that if a noun is masculine or feminine, everything around it needs to reflect that.

Not all nouns end in o or a, so here are the other endings you might see and the gender they usually are.

Words ending with *–ión, -tad, -tud and -dad are usually feminine.*

Many words ending with *-ma* or *-pa* are masculine. Even though the last letter is an *a*, you have to look at the letter right before it to make sure it's feminine.

Here are a few examples:

1. *Religión (religion) is feminine.*
2. *Felicidad (happiness)* is feminine. Let's check your pronunciation of that word. Did you say it like feh-leesee-DAD?
3. *Actitud (attitude) and amistad (friendship) are both feminine.*
4. *Mapa(map)* and problema (problem) are masculine even though they end with an a.

There are also feminine words ending in o, such as *moto, mano (hand) and foto (picture).*

Now that you know the basics of differentiating masculine and feminine, you may be asking yourself, "Does it matter if a noun is masculine or feminine?

Well, ALL the words in Spanish have to match. For example, if you are talking about a girl, you will say and write the adjectives in feminine in Spanish to match with the girl. If you are talking about a boy, same thing. You will change the ending according to the gender of the noun.

You may also find information about the gender of each word by looking it up in the dictionary.

It may seem like a lot of work initially, but you'll get used to it after some practice.

Definitive articles: the, the, the, and the

"The" is a common word used, but in Spanish there are four different forms of *the*. This doesn't have to be as complicated as it first sounds, because each form is used for different types of nouns; feminine, masculine, singular and plural.

It's especially important to know how to say "the," because it's used for almost everything. For example, in English, you might say "Juice is delicious," but in Spanish, you would say "THE juice is delicious," even if you're not talking about a specific juice carton.

Let's look at the following chart with the four different types of this word: *la, el, las,* and *los.*

	Singular	Plural
Feminine	La	Las
Masculine	El	Los

La and El

Let's start with the ones that are used to describe ONE thing.

- *La* ends with an *a*, so that's a good hint that it will be for the feminine nouns.
- *El* is a bit harder, but you'll talk about a singular, masculine noun when using it.

We just looked at these examples:
Mesa- feminine (table)
Silla- feminine (chair)
Libro- masculine (book)
Disco- masculine (disc)

Now, we don't just want to say table (mesa), we want to say THE table. *Mesa* ends with an *a*, and we know it is feminine. We are going to say la *mesa.*

La mesa- the table

LET'S PRACTICE!

Write below what 'the' you think should be used.

Feminine		Masculine	
La	mesa (table)		libro (book)
	silla (chair)		disco (disc)
	planta (plant)		equipo (team)
	manzana (apple)		producto (product)
	pelota (ball)		zapato (shoe)
	muñeca (doll)		beso (kiss)
	vida (life)		río (river)
	respuesta (answer)		edificio (building)
	carta (letter)		cuchillo (knife)
	escuela (school)		pueblo (town)

Look at the others on the list and write below what 'the' you think should be used.

Feminine		English word		Masculine	
	médica	doctor			médico
	empleada	employer			empleado
	gata	cat			gato
	perra	dog			perro
	maestra	teacher			maestro
	jugadora	player			jugador
	arquitecta	architect			arquitecto
	osa	bear			oso
	amiga	friend			amigo
	propietaria	owner			propietario

Finally, let's complete some more with little different endings. If you need to look back on the previous section to identify if a word is masculine or feminine, go ahead and do that.

	felicidad		moto
	ecosistema		actitud
	amistad		programa
	mano		televisión
	canción		síntoma
	idioma		facultad

Look at these examples: *la chica alta* (the tall girl)(notice how the words all end with 'a' to show how feminine it is) and *el chico alto* (the tall boy) (now that we're talking about a boy, we changed the adjective to end with 'o.'.)

Las and Los

Remember that there are four ways to say "the." We've only learned about two. The other two ways are used with plural nouns.

For example, instead of la *silla*, you would write *las sillas*. Because the noun became plural, anything describing the noun must also become plural.

To make nouns and adjectives plural, you should add -*s* to words ending in a vowel and -*es* to words ending in a consonant. For example *silla (chair), sillas (chairs), papel (paper), papeles (papers)*. Just know that some words change a little bit when forming the plural. For words ending in -*z*, change the *z* to *c* when adding the plural ending -*es*. For example: *lápiz, lápices (pencil, pencils)*.

LET'S PRACTICE!

Now, you have four options. Identify the correct 'the' needed for each one.

____ televisión (the TV)
____ contraseña (the password)
____ escritorios (the desks)
____ plato (the plate)
____ universidades (the universities)
____ cocinero (the cook)
____ mapa (the map)
____ motos (the motorbikes)

Congratulations! You're differentiating between masculine and feminine, singular and plural in Spanish!

Common nouns

You may learn some grammar basics, but speaking isn't enough only with grammar. You need some vocabulary too. Here is a list of some of the most commonly used nouns in Spanish with their pronunciation provided (to practice what you learned in Chapter One).

Abuela	Ah-**bweh**-lah	Grandma	Manzana	Mahn-**sah**-nah	Apple
Abuelo	Ah-**bweh**-loh	Grandpa	Marcador	Mahr-kah-**dohr**	Marker
Agua	**Ah**-gwah	Water	Mesa	**Meh**-sah	Table
Amigo	Ah-**mee**-goh	Friend	Minuto	Mee-**noo**-toh	Minute
Año	**Ah**-nyoh	Year	Mochila	Moh-**chee**-lah	Backpack
Arroz	Ah-**rrohs**	Rice	Mujer	Moo-**hehr**	Woman
Autobús	Ow-toh-**boos**	Bus	Naranja	Nah-**rahn**-jah	Orange
Avión	Ah-**byohn**	Plane	Nieve	**Nyeh**-beh	Snow
Baño	**Bah**-nyoh	Bathroom	Niño	**Nee**-nyoh	Boy
Bicicleta	Bee-see-**kleh**-tah	Bike	Oído	Oh-**ee**-doh	ear
Brazo	**Brah**-soh	Arm	Ojos	**Oh**-hohs	Eyes
Cabeza	Kah-**beh**-sah	Head	Ordenador	Ohr-deh-nah-**dohr**	Computer
Café	Kah-**feh**	Coffee	Padre	**Pah**-dreh	Father
Calendario	Kah-lehn-**dah**-ryoh	Calendar	Pan	**Pahn**	Bread
Cama	**Kah**-mah	Bed	Pantalla	Pahn-tah-**yah**	Screen
Carne	**Kahr**-neh	Meat	Parada	Pah-**rah**-dah	Stop
Carretera	Kah-rreh-**teh**-rah	Road	Pasta	**Pahs**-tah	Pasta
Carro	**Kah**-rroh	Car	Patata	Pah-**tah**-tah	Potato
Casa	**Kah**-sah	House	Pecho	**Peh**-choh	Chest
Cerveza	Sehr-**beh**-sah	Beer	Pescado	Pehs-**kah**-doh	Fish
Cocina	Koh-**see**-nah	Kitchen	Pie	**pyeh**	Foot
Contraseña	Kohn-trah-**seh**-nyha	Password	Plátano	**Plah**-tah-noh	Banana
Cuaderno	Kwah-**dehr**-noh	Notebook	Plato	**Plah**-toh	Plate
Cuchara	Koo-**chah**-rah	Spoon	Policía	Poh-lee-**see**-ah	Police
Cuchillo	Koo-**chee**-yoh	Knife	Pollo	**Poh**-yoh	Chicken
Cuenta	**Kwehn**-tah	Account	Profesor	Proh-feh-**sohr**	Teacher
Cuerpo	**Kwehr**-poh	Body	Puerta	**Pwehr**-tah	Door
Dedo	**Deh**-doh	Finger	Queso	**Keh**-soh	Cheese
Doctor	Dohk-**tohr**	Doctor	Refrigerador	Reeh-free-heh-rah-**dohr**	Refrigerator
Empresario	Ehm-preh-**sah**-ryoh	businessman	Restaurante	Rrehs-tow-**rahn**-teh	Restaurant
Enfermero	Ehn-fehr-**meh**-roh	Nurse	Secador de Pelo	Seh-kah-**dohr-deh-**peh-loh	Hairdryer

Espalda	Ehs-**pahl**-dah	Back	Segundo	Seh-**goon**-doh	Second
Espinaca	Ehs-pee-**nah**-kah	Spinach	Semáforo	Seh-**mah**-foh-roh	Traffic light
Esposa	Ehs-**poh**-sah	Wife	Semana	Seh-**mah**-nah	Week
Foto	**Foh**-toh	Photo	Silla	**See**-yah	Chair
Hermana	Ehr-**mah**-nah	Sister	Sol	**Sohl**	Sun
Hermano	Ehr-**mah**-noh	Brother	Sopa	**Soh**-pah	Soup
Hija	**ee**-hah	Daughter	Taza	**Tah**-sah	Cup
Hijo	**ee**-hoh	Son	Té	**Teh**	Tea
Hombre	**Ohm**-breh	Man	Televisión	Teh-leh-bee-**syohn**	Television
Hora	**Oh**-rah	Hour	Tenedor	Teh-neh-**dohr**	Fork
Ingeniero	Een-heh-**nyeh**-roh	Engineer	Tía	**Tee**-ah	Aunt
Lavadora	Lah-bah-**doh**-rah	Washing Machine	Tiempo	**Tyehm**-poh	Time
Leche	**Leh**-cheh	Milk	Tío	**Tee**-oh	Uncle
Lechuga	Leh-**choo**-gah	Lettuce	Tomate	Toh-**mah**-teh	Tomato
Lluvia	**Yoo**-byah	Rain	Tren	**Trehn**	Train
Luz	**Loos**	Light	Vaso	**Bah**-soh	Glass
Madre	**Mah**-dreh	Mother	Ventana	Behn-**tah**-nah	Window
Maestra	Mah-**ehs**-trah	Teacher	Ventilador	Behn-tee-lah-**dohr**	Fan
Mano	**Mah**-noh	Hand	Vino	**Bee**-noh	Wine

LET'S PRACTICE!

Review

Subject pronouns

How do you refer to…? ¿Cómo le dirías a…

1. Your best friend? _____
2. Two or more female teachers? _____
3. Two or more boys? _____
4. Your mother? _____
5. The President of your country? _____
6. A group of female and male tourists? _____
7. A group of female soccer players? _____
8. Yourself? _____
9. Your family? _____
10. Your uncle? _____

Feminine or masculine?
Recognize each gender and complete the table below using la or el:

Oso	Perro	Mesa	Saco

Planta	Manzana	Huevo	Baño

Gata	Silla

Feminine	Masculine

Now please, set the same list in the plural forms using las or los:

Let's review the use of *el, la, los,* and *las*. Connect with lines

El	•	•	mochila
Los	•	•	comidas
La	•	•	perro
La	•	•	tarea
Las	•	•	patos

Nouns need adjectives to give them more detail, whether that's a color or emotion. To build up our phrases, we will look at how to use adjectives in Spanish in this next chapter.

CHAPTER 4

DEMONSTRATIVE AND POSSESSIVE ARTICLES, ADJECTIVES AND DESCRIBING HOW YOU FEEL

Demonstrative articles

There are twelve demonstrative articles in Spanish:

- Este or esta and their plural forms estos or estas refer to near things (this and these). The first series implies closeness or immediacy according to the speaker. Esta mujer (this woman), este libro (this book), estas niñas (these girls), estos árboles (these trees).
- Ese and esa and their plural forms esos and esas refer to the things that are not near nor far away (that and those). The second series implies a certain distance from the speaker. Ese perro (that dog), esa casa (that house), esos carros (those cars), esas tiendas (those shops)
- Aquel and aquella and their plural forms aquellos and aquellas refer to things that can have a bigger physical, temporal or any kind of separation. Aquel año (that year), aquella pintura (that painting), aquellos soldados (those soldiers), aquellos planetas (those planets)

Este o esta	Ese o esa	Aquel o aquella
Estos o estas	Esos o esas	Aquellos o aquellas

Possessive articles

The possessive articles establish a relationship of belonging or possession with the noun and always appear before or after it.

Personal pronoun	Before the noun		After the noun	
	Singular	Plural	Singular	Plural
Yo	mi	mis	mío/mía	míos/mías
Tú	tu	tus	tuyo/tuya	tuyos/tuyas
Él/ella	su	sus	suyo/suya	suyos/suyas
Usted	su	sus	suyo/suya	suyos/suyas
Nosotros/nosotras	nuestro/nuestra	nuestros/nuestra	nuestro/nuestra	nuestros/nuestra
Vosotros/vosotras	vuestro/vuestras	vuestros/vuestras	vuestro/vuestras	vuestros/vuestras
Ellos/ellas	su	sus	suyo/suya	suyos/suyas
Ustedes	su	sus	suyo/suya	suyos/suyas

Examples

Personal pronoun	Before the noun		After the noun	
	Singular	Plural	Singular	Plural
Yo	Mi amigo	mis amigos	amigo mío/ amiga mía	amigos míos/ amigas mías
Tú	Tu madre	Tus hermanas	Regalo tuyo/ gata tuya	Papeles tuyos/ camisas tuyas

Adjectives

Adjectives are grammatical elements that give characteristics to people, animals, or things. They provide extra information about the nouns. Beautiful, sweet, hard, long, and yellow are adjectives. Different types or categories of adjectives are used daily to highlight the characteristics or determine the nouns to which we refer. (qualitative, numeral, demonym among others)

Here is a list of some common adjectives. Notice that some of the words below have a letter in parentheses. That means the word can change whether you talk about a masculine or feminine noun. Do you remember which letter you would use for a masculine noun? The stressed syllable is underlined for you to practice pronunciation as well.

Abierto(a)	Open	Ah-**beeehr**-toh	Holgado(a)	Loose, baggy	Ohl-**gah**-doh
Aburrido(a)	Boring	Ah-boo-**rree**-doh	Importante	Important	Eem-pohr-**tahn**-the
Afortunado(a)	Lucky	Ah-fohr-too-**nah**-doh	Inteligente	Intelligent	Een-teh-lee-**hehn**-the
Agradable	Pleasant	Ah-grah-**dah**-bleh	Interesante	Interesting	Een-teh-reh-**sahn**-the
Alto(a)	High	**Ahl**-toh	Inútil	Useless	ee-**noo**-teel
Alto(a)	Tall	**Ahl**-toh	Joven	Young	**Hoh**-behn
Amable	Friendly	Ah-**mah**-bleh	Largo(a)	Long	**Lahr**-goh
Amargo(a)	Bitter	Ah-**mahr**-goh	Lejos	Far	**Leh**-hohs
Amigable	Friendly	Ah-mee-**gah**-bleh	Lento(a)	Slow	**Lehn**-toh
Ancho(a)	Wide	**Ahn**-choh	Ligero(a)	Light	Lee-**heh**-roh
Apretado	Tight	Ah-preh-**tah**-doh	Limpio(a)	Clean	**Leem**-pyoh
Bajo(a)	Low	**Bah**-hoh	Lleno(a)	Full	**Yeh**-noh
Barato(a)	Cheap	Bah-**rah**-toh	Loco(a)	Crazy	**Loh**-koh
Blando(a)	Soft	**Blahn**-doh	Luminoso (a)	Bright	Loo-mee-**noh**-soh
Bonito(a)	Nice, pretty	Boh-**nee**-toh	Mal educado(a)	Rude	Mahl-eh-doo-**kah**-doh
Bueno(a)	Good	**Bweh**-noh	Malo(a)	Bad	**Mah**-loh
Caliente	Hot	Kah-**lyehn**-the	Mojado(a)	Wet	Moh-**hah**-doh

Spanish	English	Pronunciation	Spanish	English	Pronunciation
Caro(a)	Expensive	**Kah**-roh	Muchos(as)	Many	**Moo**-chos
Cerca	Near	**Sehr**-kah	Muerto(a)	Dead	**Mwehr**-toh
Cerrado(a)	Closed , shut	Seh-**rrah**-doh	Nuevo(a)	New	**Nweh**-boh
Correcto(a)	Right, correct	Koh-**rrehk**-toh	Oscuro(a)	Dark	Ohs-**koo**-roh
Corto(a)	Short	**Kohr**-toh	Peligroso(a)	Dangerous	Peh-lee-**groh**-soh
Delgado(a)	Thin, slim, lean	Dehl-**gah**-doh	Pequeño(a)	Small	Peh-**keh**-nyoh
Débil	Weak	**Deh**-beel	Pesado(a)	Heavy	Peh-**sah**-doh
Desafortunado (a)	Unlucky	Deh-sah-fohr-too-**nah**-doh	Petizo(a)	Short	Peh-**tee**-soh
Desagradable	Unpleasant	Deh-sah-grah-**dah**-bleh	Pobre	Poor	**Poh**-breh
Difícil	Difficult, hard	Dee-**fee**-seel	Pocos(as)	Few	**Poh**-kos
Divertido(a)	Fun	Dee-behr-**tee**-doh	Preocupado(a)	Worried	Preh-oh-koo-**pah**-doh
Dulce	Sweet	**Dool**-seh	Profundo(a)	Deep	Proh-foon-doh
Duro(a)	Hard	**Doo**-roh	Rápido(a)	Fast	**Rrah**-pee-doh
Educado(a)	Polite	Eh-doo-**kah**-doh	Relajado(a)	Relaxed	Rreh-lah-**hah**-doh
Emocionado(a)	Excited	Eh-moh-syoh-**nah**-doh	Rico(a)	Rich	**Rree**-koh
Enfermo	Sick	Ehn-**fehr**-moh	Ruidoso(a)	Loud	Rrwee-**doh**-soh
Enojado(a)	Angry	Eh-noh-**hah**-doh	Seco(a)	Dry	**Seh**-koh
Equivocado(a)	Wrong	Eh-kee-boh-**kah**-doh	Seguro(a)	Safe	Seh-**goo**-roh
Estrecho(a)	Narrow	Ehs-**treh**-choh	Sincero(a)	Sincere	Seen-**seh**-roh
Estúpido(a)	Stupid	Ehs-**too**-pee-doh	Sucio(a)	Dirty	**Soo**-syoh
Excelente	Excellent	Ehk-se-**lehn**-teh	Superficial	Shallow	Soo-pehr-**fee**-syal
Fácil	Easy	**Fah**-seel	Tacaño(a)	Stingy	Tah-**kah**-nyoh
Falso(a)	False	**Fahl**-soh	Tarde	Late	**Tahr**-deh
Feliz	Happy	Feh-**lees**	Temprano	Early	Tehm-**prah**-noh
Feo(a)	Ugly	**Feh**-oh	Terrible	Terrible	Teh-**rree**-bleh
Fino(a)	Thin	**Fee**-noh	Tímido(a)	Shy	**Tee**-mee-doh
Frío(a)	Cold	**Free**-oh	Tranquilo (a)	Quiet	Trahn-**kee**-loh
Fuerte	Strong	**Fwehr**-teh	Triste	Sad	**Trees**-the
Generoso(a)	Generous	Heh-neh-**roh**-soh	Útil	Useful	**oo**-teel
Gordo(a)	Fat	**Gohr**-doh	Vacío(a)	Empty	Bah-**see**-oh
Grande	Big	**Grahn**-deh	Verdadero(a)	True	Behr-dah-**deh**-roh
Grueso(a)	Thick	**Grweh**-soh	Viejo(a)	Old	**Byeh**-hoh
Hermoso(a)	Beautiful	Ehr-**moh**-soh	Violento	Violent	Byoh-**lehn**-toh

It's important to remember that many adjectives in Spanish (except for numbers, some possessive adjectives like *mi, tu, nuestro* and demonstrative adjectives, such as *this and that*) come AFTER the noun they modify.

Just like nouns and articles, adjectives can change too. They follow the same pattern, and we must modify them if the noun is feminine, masculine, singular or plural.

For example, *the blue house is la casa azul* (the house blue).

However, if you want to say the **six houses**, you would say *las seis casas.*

Read these examples

- El libro viejo - the old book

- Las sillas grandes- the big chairs

- Los perros gordos- the fat dogs

- La cama blanda- the soft bed

- La silla grande- the big chair

- El libro grande- the big book

Even though silla is feminine and libro is masculine, grande can describe both without changing. This adjective can become plural, however.

- Las sillas grandes- the big chairs (more than one chair)

- Los libros grandes- the big books (more than one book)

LET´S PRACTICE!

Set the singular or plural of the following parts:

	Las espinacas frías
Una lavadora grande	
	Esas tazas calientes
El tomate pequeño	
	Unos niños terribles
Mi amigo preocupado	
	Los carros limpios

Now...it is time to combine articles, nouns, and adjectives.
You can read the following phrases out loud and connect with the meaning:

Ese cuaderno útil •	• My stingy friends
Tu dedo fino •	• That cold fish
Mi carro sucio •	• The strong arm
Aquellos ojos mojados •	• Your thin finger
El autobus rápido •	• That useful notebook
El brazo fuerte •	• Those wet eyes
Ese pescado frío •	• Her quiet house
Mis amigas tacañas •	• Their full spoons
Sus cucharas llenas •	• The fast bus
Su casa tranquila •	• My dirty car

Let's do it one more time!

Tus ojos bonitos •	• Our clean kitchen
Mi plato pequeño •	• Your beautiful eyes
Esa bicicleta pesada •	• That bright window
Aquella puerta oscura •	• My small plate
Nuestra cocina limpia •	• This polite boy
Esa taza caliente •	• This hot cup
Este niño educado •	• That dark door
Aquella ventana luminosa •	• That closed restaurant
Esta nieve blanda •	• This heavy bicycle
Aquel restaurante cerrado •	• This soft snow

Once again, because it doesn't end in an 'a' or an 'o,' you can use it to describe masculine and feminine things without changing. However, when it becomes plural, you add 'es' instead of just 's.'

Take a look at these examples.

- La persona débil- the weak person
- Las personas débiles- the weak people

- La clase fácil- the easy class
- Las clases fáciles- the easy classes

These are the basic rules for changing the endings of adjectives. The following chart summarizes the most common endings for feminine or masculine, or both forms.

Masculine	Feminine	Masculine and Feminine
-o bonito, favorito	**-a** bonita, favorita	**-e** grande, dulce
-és inglés, francés	**-esa** inglesa, francesa	**-a** (some exceptions) indígena, hipócrita
-án, -ín, -ón,-or charlatán, glotón, trabajador	**-ana, -ina, -ona,-ora** charlatana, glotona, trabajadora	**In consonants** (different from -ín, -án, -ón, -or) difícil, feliz

More vocabulary

Aburrido/a	(ah-boo-rree-doh)	Boring
Activo/a	(ahk-tee-boh)	Active
Antipático/a	(ahn-tee-pah-tee-koh)	Unfriendly
Trabajador/a	(trah-bah-hah-dohr)	Hardworking
Inteligente	(een-teh-lee-hehn-teh	Smart
Extrovertido/a	(ehks-troh-behr-tee-doh)	Outgoing
Tonto/a	(tohn-toh)	Silly
Simpático/a	(seem-pah-tee-koh)	Friendly

Describing how you feel

In Chapter 2, we have introduced feelings like estoy feliz and estoy enfermo that allow you to express whether you are happy or sick. However, the Spanish language is so rich that a large variety of feelings and emotions can show you different contexts and they're deeply rooted in Spanish culture. If someone wants to begin a conversation with you there are many ways to start and answer. Get ready!

¿Cómo estás?	How are you?
¿Cómo te sientes?	How do you feel?
¿Cómo andas?	How are you doing?
¿Te sientes cansado?	Do you feel tired?"
¿Qué te sucede?	What´s wrong?
Estoy muy bien	I am very good
Me siento triste	I feel sad
Estoy bien./Ando bien.	I am good. I am doing good.
Estoy exhausto.	I am exhausted
No me pasa nada	Nothing is wrong
Me siento frustrado	I feel frustrated
Estoy preocupado	I am worried

Here is a list of some common feelings

Aburrido	(ah-boo-rree-doh)	Boring
Agobiado	(ah-goh-byah-doh)	Overwhelmed
Agradecido	(ah-grah-deh-see-doh)	Grateful
Alegre	(ah-leh-greh)	Happy
Aliviado	(ah-lee-beeah-doh)	Relieved
Amargado	(ah-mahr-gah-doh)	Bitter
Ansioso	(ahn-syoh-soh)	Anxious
Asustado	(ah-soos-tah-doh)	Scared
Avergonzado	(ah-behr-gohn-sah-doh)	Ashamed
Cansado	(kahn-sah-doh)	Tired
Celoso	(seh-loh-soh)	Jealous
Cómodo	(koh-moh-doh)	Comfortable
Confundido	(kohn-foon-dee-doh)	Confused
Contento	(kohn-tehn-toh)	Happy
Deprimido	(deh-pree-mee-doh)	Depressed

Desesperado	(dehs-ehs-peh-rah-doh)	Desperate
Dolido	(dehs-ehs-peh-rah-doh)	Hurt
Emocionado	(eh-moh-syoh-nah-doh)	Excited
Enamorado	(eh-nah-moh-rah-doh)	In love
Encantado	(ehn-kahn-tah-doh)	Delighted
Enfadado	(ehn-phah-dah-doh)	Angry
Envidioso	(ehn-bee-dyoh-soh)	Envious
Estresado	(ehs-treh-sah-doh)	Stressed
Fascinado	(fah-see-nah-doh)	Fascinated
Feliz	(feh-lees)	Happy
Frustrado	(froos-trah-doh)	Frustrated
Furioso	(foo-ryoh-soh)	Furious
Impaciente	(eem-pah-syehn-teh)	Impatient
Incómodo	(eeng-koh-moh-doh)	Uncomfortable
Infeliz	(een-feh-lees)	Unhappy
Inquieto	(eeng-kyeh-toh)	Restless
Inseguro	(een-seh-goo-roh)	Insecure
Malhumorado	(mahl-oo-moh-rah-doh)	Grumpy
Molesto	(moh-lehs-toh)	Annoying
Nervioso	(nehr-byoh-soh)	Nervous
Nostálgico	(nohs-tahl-hee-koh)	Nostalgic
Ocupado	(oh-koo-pah-doh)	Busy
Optimista	(ohp-tee-mees-tah)	Hopeful
Orgulloso	(ohr-goo-yoh-soh)	Proud
Paciente	(pah-syehn-teh)	Patient
Pesimista	(peh-see-mees-tah)	Pessimist
Preocupado	(preh-oh-koo-pah-doh)	Worried
Relajado	(rreh-lah-hah-doh)	Relaxed
Satisfecho	(sah-tees-feh-choh)	Satisfied
Sensible	(sehn-see-bleh)	Sensitive
Sorprendido	(sohr-prehn-dee-doh)	Surprised
Tímido	(tee-mee-doh)	Shy
Triste	(trees-teh)	Sad

CHAPTER 5

SER AND ESTAR

We have learned about some adjectives, nouns, and pronouns.

In this chapter we will study the verb "to be", and we will be able to start building simple sentences. The verb to be, has two different froms: ser and estar. They are used quite differently. Both are irregular verbs. Like in English, they both follow the patterns shown below in the present tense.

English	Pronoun	Ser		Estar	
I am	Yo	Soy	(Sohee)	Estoy	(Ehs-toy)
You are	Tú	Eres	(Eh-rehs)	Estás	(Ehs-tahs)
He/she is	Él/ella/usted	Es	(ehs)	Está	(Ehs-tah)
We are	Nosotros/as	Somos	(Soh-mohs)	Estamos	(Ehs-tah-mohs)
You are	Vosotros/as	Sois	(Soh-is)	Estáis	(Ehs-tahis)
They are	Ellos/ellas/ustedes	Son	Sohn	Están	(Hs-than)

Ser

Let's look at the specific uses and a few examples.

1. *Defining Characteristics and Definitions*- If you're describing someone, saying he is tall or she is interesting, then you would use ser.

   - Él es alto- He is tall
   - Ella es interesante- She is interesting
   - Nosotros somos artísticos- We are artistic.
   - Ellos son trabajadores. - They are workers.
   - Un mono es un animal. -A monkey is an animal.

We are describing these people, so we use a version of the word ser.

2. *Profession, Name, or Relationship*- If you introduce yourself or someone else, you use ser.

   - Yo soy maestra- I am a teacher.
   - Ustedes son estudiantes- You all are students.
   - Ellos son mis amigos- They are my friends.

In all of these examples, someone has a certain role or job to play, even if that is being a friend. You can also use it to say someone is a man, woman, child, etc.

3. *Point of Origin-* To tell where someone is from (using countries or nationalities), you use *ser.*

  - Mis amigos son de Puerto Rico- My friends are from Puerto Rico.
  - Nosotros somos de los Estados Unidos- We are from the United States.
  - Tú eres de aquí- You are from here.
  - Ellos son franceses- They are French.

4. *Ownership-* If we say something is his, hers, ours, etc., then we use a version of ser. Note that in Spanish, we cannot use 's to show someone's ownership. In English, we might say this is John's book. In Spanish, you need to say "This is the book of John," "the backpack of Julia," and "the father of María."

  - Este lápiz es de Nora- This pencil is Nora's.
  - La mochila es de ellos- The backpack is theirs.
  - Estos son los padres de Marcos- These are Marco's parents
  - Mi familia es muy grande- My family is very big

5. *Material-* If you tell what something is made of, you will use *ser.*

  - La casa es de madera- The house is made of wood.
  - Las mochilas son de algodón- The backpacks are made from cotton.

6. *Time and date-* If you're telling time, you always use "son" for two o'clock or after and "es" for one o'clock.

  - Es la una.- It's one ó clock.
  - Son las tres. - It's three o'clock.
  - Son las ocho. - It's eight o'clock.
  - Es lunes. - It's Monday.
  - Es verano. - It's summer.

7. *Events-* If you're talking about the place, time, and date an event is taking place, you use *ser.*

  - La fiesta es en mi casa. - The party is at my place.
  - La boda es en marzo. - The wedding is in March.

Yo	soy	I am
Tú	eres	You are
Él/ella/usted	es	He/she is
Nosotros/as	somos	We are
Vosotros/as	sois	You are
Ellos/ellas/ustedes	son	They are

Match the pronouns and the rest of the sentences with lines.

Yo •	• son niños
Nosotras •	• es un doctor
Ellos •	• son muy generosas
Tú •	• eres mi amigo
Ellas •	• es mi hermano
Él •	• son mexicanos
Usted •	• somos cantantes
Ustedes •	• soy estudiante

Nosotros •	• es un deportista
Ella •	• soy ingeniera
Ustedes •	• es alto
Él •	• son inteligentes
Yo •	• eres cocinera
Ellos •	• somos hermanos
Tú •	• es de Colombia
Usted •	• son amables

Complete the sentences with the missing verb.

Ellos _____ mis hermanos. (They are my brothers.)

Nuestros abuelos son de Madrid, _____ españoles. (Our grandparents are from Madrid, they are Spanish.)

_____ eres muy inteligente. (You're very smart.)

_____ las cinco de la tarde. (It's 5 p. m.)

Esta _____ una blusa de seda. (This is a silk blouse.)

Nosotros _____ muy puntuales. (We are very punctual.)

Estos dos libros _____ de José. (These two books belong to José.)

La fiesta _____ en la casa de Marta. (The party is at Marta's house.)

Let´s find the verbs in the correct form but one step harder. This time you will have to use all your Spanish knowledge. Get ready!

Pablo …… de Jamaica y su amigo Joaquín …… de Colombia. Nosotros …… una familia. Yo …… de México y mi mamá y mi papá …… de Ecuador. Mi hermano Raúl……de Texas. Él …… un ingeniero y su mochila …… azul. Este …… mi hijo pequeño. Su nombre …… Diego y su cuaderno …… grande. Mi teléfono…… 1-957-11-23-40-00. ¡Adiós! ¡Te veo pronto!

It is time to write complete sentences for the first time.

Yo	Gaby	Teléfono	1-954-20-34-12-23
Tú	Washington	Gata	Frida
Él	arquitecto	Productos	muy buenos
Nosotros	profesores	José y María	alumnos
Ellos	médicos	Ambulancia	blanca

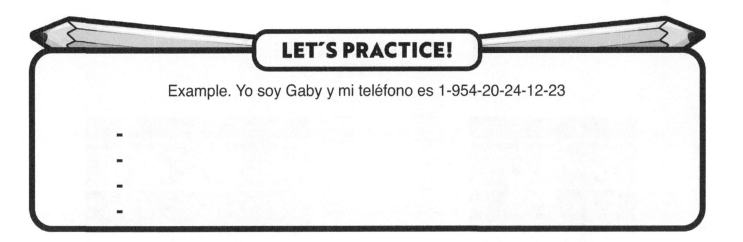

Example. Yo soy Gaby y mi teléfono es 1-954-20-24-12-23

-
-
-
-

Estar

The other meaning of the verb to be is estar and it is used in Spanish when:

1. Generally, we use estar to talk about *temporary states or conditions.* So, if you are going to talk about feelings, then you would use estar, because it's a changeable condition. The same goes for health conditions, or other unstable states such as weather conditions, and general circumstances.

   - Yo estoy feliz. - I'm happy.
   - Mi hermano está enfermo. - My brother is sick.
   - El día está caluroso. – The day is hot.
   - Carlos está muy ocupado. - Carlos is very busy.
   - La estación de trenes está llena de gente. - The train station is full of people.

2. Another common use of *estar* is for locations, except when you're talking about events! (see above, item 7)

   - Mi casa está en un vecindario tranquilo. - (My house is in a quiet neighborhood.)
   - La tienda está al lado del bar. - (The store is next to the bar.)

3. You may also use *estar* when describing feelings perceived by the five senses.

   - La música está muy fuerte. - The music is too loud.
   - La sopa está fría. - The soup is cold.
   - Las tiendas están cerradas. The stores are closed.

Yo	estoy	I am
Tú	estás	You are
Él/ella/usted	está	He/she is
Nosotros/as	estamos	We are
Vosotros/as	estáis	You are
Ellos/ellas/ustedes	están	They are

Complete the following sentences with the correct form of the verb to be.

Ella		en Uruguay.
Ellos		en la ciudad de San Francisco.
Nosotros		en una fiesta.
Él		enfermo.
Nosotros		preocupados.
Yo		muy feliz.
Ustedes		cansados.
Tú		hambriento.
Chile		en América del Sur.
Pedro		en el juego de fútbol.
Marina y Andrea		en el cine.

Rewrite the sentence with the subject pronoun in front. Look at this example.
Estamos cansados- Nosotros estamos cansados.

Note: Because nosotros is the only pronoun that matches the '-amos' ending, we know this sentence must be talking about them. Some verb forms match with more than one person so you may choose any option.

Están en la casa. - _____

Estás bien. - _____

Está en la cama. _____

Estamos cerca. _____

Está enojada. _____

Estoy triste. _____

Estar and Ser Practice

Now that you've had the chance to learn both verbs and conjugations, let's do some practice. Translate the following sentences into Spanish.

The girl is happy. _____

They are friends. _____

We are from the United States. _____

I am tall. _____

You are tired. _____

He is smart. _____

It is difficult. _____

The parents are in the house. _____

Match with lines to make the perfect sentences.

Luis •	• somos estudiantes de Física
La luna •	• soy de Mississippi
María y Julieta •	• están en un partido de fútbol
Mi hermano y yo •	• es alto y moreno.
El Presidente de los Estados Unidos •	• está por la noche
Yo •	• están en la tienda de juguetes
Los niños •	• es una niña muy atenta
El carro de José •	• está en su avión
Julia •	• eres muy gracioso
Yo •	• estamos solos en la casa
El profesor González •	• es gris
Tú •	• estoy muy cansado
Pedro y yo •	• es en Febrero
Las pelotas de golf •	• son blancas
El cumpleaños de Tomás •	• está muy ocupado

Finally, focus on the different uses of *ser* and *estar* and choose one of the two verbs.

- El café **(es - está)** muy caliente. The coffee is too hot.
- Mi bicicleta **(es - está)** rota. My bike is broken.
- Tu cumpleaños **(es - está)** el 3 de enero. Your birthday is on January 3rd.
- Estos zapatos **(son - están)** de cuero. These are leather shoes.
- Ella **(es - está)** mi mejor amiga. She is my best friend.
- Este carro **(es - está)** muy rápido. This car is very fast.
- Nosotros **(somos - estamos)** de viaje. We are on a trip.
- El desfile **(es - está)** en el parque. The parade is in the park.
- Ustedes **(son - están)** colombianos. You're Colombians.
- **(Soy - Estoy)** muy resfriado. I have a cold.
- Las verduras **(son - están)** muy saludables. Vegetables are very healthy.

CHAPTER 6

INTRODUCING VERBS

Verbs are words that carry the action in a sentence. So, knowing how to use verbs properly in Spanish will help you create many different sentences from the beginning. What do you know about verbs already?

Verbs vary in tense, aspect, mood, voice, number, and person. In Spanish, every verb has a stem and an ending. The stem gives us the verb´s meaning. The infinitive endings in Spanish are three: ar-er and ir. Verbs change their ending depending on whom they are talking about. Think of the verb ending changes as "matching" the verb to the subject pronoun. Remember that when you use a conjugated verb, you can use it WITH the pronoun or WITHOUT it.

The verb you learned to conjugate in chapter 5- estar- is almost regular. Just the first form- yo- is irregular. You will see the same endings repeated here. Looking at the end of a verb will tell you how to conjugate it.

Verb List

This is a list of a few verbs and their meanings before we learn how to conjugate them. There are different tenses in Spanish. By now, we will focus on the present tense. Keep in mind that all of the verbs on this list are regular and won't break the conjugation rules we are learning.

ar		er		ir	
Cocinar	to cook	correr	to run	vivir	to live
Descansar	to rest	beber	to drink	escribir	to write
Caminar	to walk	comer	to eat	unir	to unit
Escuchar	to listen	vender	to sell	abrir	to open
Comprar	to buy	aprender	to learn	cubrir	to cover
Hablar	to talk	barrer	to sweep	dividir	to divide
Montar	to ride	coger	to catch	debatir	to debate
Estudiar	to study	acceder	to access	decidir	to decide
Trabajar	to work	comprender	to understand	permitir	to allow
Limpiar	to clean	depender	to rely	subir	to go up
Cantar	to sing	desprender	to detach	describir	to describe
Nadar	to swim	esconder	to hide	compartir	to share
Patinar	to skate	romper	to break	recibir	to receive
Tocar	to play	toser	to cough	aplaudir	to clap

Circle the stem and cross the ending of each verb

coser	dormir	cocinar	medir	soltar
jugar	estar	trabajar	saltar	temer
estornudar	comer	manejar	permitir	estordunar
tener	tocar	mover	cavar	prohibir
caer	sentir	conducir	servir	abolir

When the verb combines with a subject, conjugation occurs. To conjugate a regular verb in the present tense, just take out the infinitive ar-er-ir and add the ending that matches the subject.

-AR Verbs

Let´s see the present tense conjugation of a regular verb that finishes with ar. For example: caminar (to walk). The stem is camin and the ending finishes according to the subject. All regular verbs with an ar ending are similar.

Yo	camino	Nosotros	caminamos
Tú	caminas	Ustedes	Caminan
Ella/él/usted	camina	Ellos/ellas	Caminan

Note that the changes are just in the ENDINGS. To form the new conjugation, you need to remove the -ar ending and replace it with the ending that matches your pronoun. Let's look at an example with hablar (this is a verb that means 'to talk' in Spanish).

Yo	hablo	Nosotros	hablamos
Tú	hablas	Ustedes	hablan
Ella/él/usted	habla	Ellos/ellas	hablan

We will study the verb hablar (to speak) and take out the -ar ending. That leaves us with the root- habl-. Now, we can add the endings in the first chart onto the end of habl-.

We can do this with another -ar verb.

Yo	estudio	Nosotros	estudiamos
Tú	estudias	Ustedes	estudian
Ella/él/usted	estudia	Ellos/ellas	estudian

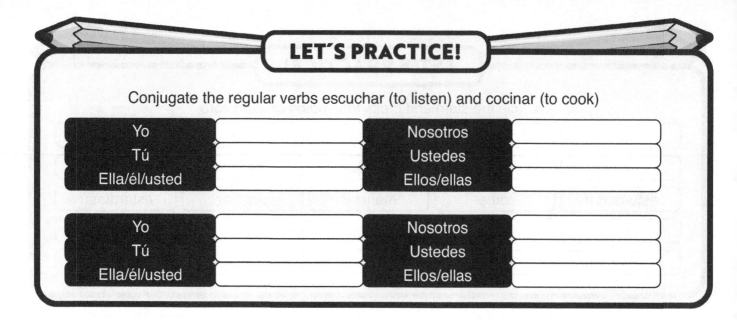

Conjugate the regular verbs escuchar (to listen) and cocinar (to cook)

Yo		Nosotros	
Tú		Ustedes	
Ella/él/usted		Ellos/ellas	

Yo		Nosotros	
Tú		Ustedes	
Ella/él/usted		Ellos/ellas	

-ER Verbs

The present tense conjugation of a regular verb that finishes with er is very similar to the one we studied before, for example comer (to eat). The stem is com and the ending finishes according to the subject. All regular verbs with an er ending are similar.

Yo	com**o**	Nosotros	com**emos**
Tú	com**es**	Ustedes	com**en**
Ella/él/usted	com**e**	Ellos/ellas	com**en**

What do you notice is different and similar between the two endings? The vowels are different, but the basic ending stays the same.

Let's study another one. The verb beber (to drink) Look at this example more closely.

Yo	beb**o**	Nosotros	beb**emos**
Tú	beb**es**	Ustedes	beb**en**
Ella/él/usted	beb**e**	Ellos/ellas	beb**en**

Now, we can make lots of sentences about eating and drinking.

Ella come fruta.- She eats fruit.
Nosotros comemos verduras. We eat vegetables.
Él bebe agua. He drinks water.
Ustedes beben jugo. You drink juice.

Conjugate the regular verbs aprender (to learn) and correr (to run)

Yo		Nosotros	
Tú		Ustedes	
Ella/él/usted		Ellos/ellas	

Yo		Nosotros	
Tú		Ustedes	
Ella/él/usted		Ellos/ellas	

-IR Verbs

-IR endings are the last set. Compare the endings below to the chart above. Let´s see the verb escribir (to write)

Yo	escrib**o**	Nosotros	escrib**imos**
Tú	escrib**es**	Ustedes	escrib**en**
Ella/él/usted	escrib**e**	Ellos/ellas	escrib**en**

The only difference between *-er* and *-ir* is the *nosotros* conjugation. Let's look at one more chart showing how *vivir (to live)*, an *-ir* verb, would look conjugated.

Yo	viv**o**	Nosotros	viv**imos**
Tú	viv**es**	Ustedes	viv**en**
Ella/él/usted	viv**e**	Ellos/ellas	viv**en**

Conjugate the regular verbs subir (to go up) and abrir (to open)

Yo		Nosotros	
Tú		Ustedes	
Ella/él/usted		Ellos/ellas	

Yo		Nosotros	
Tú		Ustedes	
Ella/él/usted		Ellos/ellas	

Moving forward, remember that all you need is the person and the conjugated verb to make a complete sentence.

Conjugation Practice

Using the conjugation tips, you have just learned, change the verb to match the person. For extra practice, write the meaning afterward.

Yo/ estudiar _____

Ellos/ comprar _____

Nosotros/ vivir _____

Tú/ hablar _____

Usted/ comer _____

Los niños/ montar _____

Yo/ escribir _____

Él/ hablar _____

Tú y yo/ beber _____

Complete the sentences with the correct verbs.

vives – escucho – leemos – paga – bailo – lee –
comen – corres – escribimos – abre – beben – corro

1. Mis amigos y yo ……………………………cartas a nuestras familias.
2. Manuela y Laura ………………………… café en un bar.
3. Yo …………………….por el parque todos los días.
4. Nicolás y Manuel ……………………….pizza en un restaurante
5. Tú ………………….en la calle Hudson.
6. Mi abuela……….muchos libros.
7. Yo …………………….canciones de rock.
8. La tienda de comida ………………….a las 11 de la mañana.
9. Yo …………………….con Pablo.
10. Tú………………….muy rápido.
11. Él……………………….la entrada de cine.
12. Nosotros……………………………….El Quijote de la Mancha.

Let's conjugate the verbs in the right way!

1. ¡Pedro es muy inteligente! _____ (hablar) inglés, francés, alemán y un poco de mandarín.
2. ¿_____ (bajar, ellos) por la escalera de incendios?
3. ¿Qué _____ (estudiar, tú)?
4. ¿_____ (desayunar, nosotros) juntos?
5. Tus padres_____ (escuchar) a todos.
6. ¿Dónde _____ (trabajar, ellos)?
7. Mi hermana _____ (vivir) muy cerca de la universidad.
8. Tú_____ (comprender) a tus hijos.
9. Ella _____ (bailar) muy bien.
10. Él _____(cocinar) para un restaurante.

Write your own sentences.
Choose the words from each column to create your own sentences.

María y yo	cocinar pasteles	todos los días
Los niños	pasear por las tiendas	los domingos
Pedro y Carlos	estudiar italiano	por la noche
El amigo de José	practicar deportes	los viernes
La Señora García	tocar el piano	los lunes
Ustedes	comer pasta	los sábados y domingos
Yo	trabajar en la oficina	de lunes a viernes
Ella	mirar películas	después de la escuela

Example: La Señora García trabaja en la oficina de lunes a viernes.

....

....

....

....

....

....

....

The verbs that we have been studying are all regular ones. This is because they have a predictable pattern to be conjugated.

CHAPTER 7

IRREGULAR VERBS

Even though it would be nice if all the verbs could follow the same patterns, some are different. Below is a list of the most commonly used irregular verbs and their conjugations.

Ir- to go.

Yo	voy	Nosotros	vamos
Tú	vas	Ustedes	van
Ella/él/usted	va	Ellos/ellas	van

You can see that even though this verb has a completely different root from the base form, it still follows most of the regular endings. When you are talking about going to a place, you need "a" which means 'to.'

Read these example sentences.

Yo voy a la casa. I go to the house.
Ellos van a la escuela. They go to the school.

Here is a list of a few common places (nouns) to learn.
- La escuela- The school
- La tienda- store
- La biblioteca- library
- El cine- movie theater
- La piscina- pool
- La casa de _____- _____´s house ( ) _____

Look at how we can demonstrate ownership in the following examples.

I go to my friend's house- Yo voy a la casa de mi amigo.
We go to our grandma's house- Vamos a la casa de nuestra abuela.

Instead of 's, we say the house of my friend or the house of our grandmother.

Another irregular verb is jugar (to play a game or a sport)

Yo	juego	Nosotros	jugamos
Tú	juegas	Ustedes	juegan
Ella/él/usted	juega	Ellos/ellas	juegan

Connect with lines to create sentences.

Mi amigo y yo •	• juega fútbol en el parque con sus amigos
Nosotras •	• voy a la casa de mi amigo Pedro
Julieta y Pablo •	• jugamos ajedrez en la casa de mi abuela
Ella •	• vamos de compras los fines de semana
Yo •	• juegan béisbol profesionalmente
Ustedes •	• van a la biblioteca en el tiempo libre
Los maestros de mi escuela •	• van a la piscina en verano
Ellos •	• van a la playa los sábados y domingos

Quick Talk about the Future

Another neat thing about the verb 'ir' is you can use it to talk about the future or things you are GOING to do. You follow this pattern when making sentences.

Conjugated version of ir (to go) + a + unconjugated verb

- Yo voy a estudiar- I am going to study.
- Mis amigos van a hablar español- My friends are going to speak Spanish.
- Él va a comer fruta. He is going to eat fruit.

LET'S PRACTICE!

Write three sentences about things you plan to do this week. Remember that you can always look up some new words, but here are a few prompts to get you started.

Pasar un rato con los amigos- to hang out with friends
Mirar televisión- to watch TV
Visitar- to visit
Manejar- to drive

_____
_____
_____

The next set of irregular verbs all follow one rule (even though they don't follow the regular rules, they at least follow a different one).

These verbs can be grouped and called "yo-go" verbs, because the "yo" version of the verb ends with "go" instead of just "o."

Verbs that follow this rule are
Tener- to have
Hacer- to do or to make
Poner- to put
Venir- to come
Traer- to bring
Decir- to say

Some of these change their spelling slightly, so we'll give each one its chart. Read the verbs aloud and add a word or two to the end of each pronoun and verb to make a little sentence.

- Verb tener (to have)

Yo	tengo	Nosotros	tenemos
Tú	tienes	Ustedes	tienen
Ella/él/usted	tiene	Ellos/ellas	tienen

Notice that this verb also has an 'i' added into the root for the *tú, él/ ella/ usted,* and *ellos/ ustedes* conjugations. We can make sentences about things we have.

Yo tengo una casa. - I have a house.
Nosotros tenemos un libro de español. - We have a Spanish book.
Ellos tienen cinco mascotas. - They have five pets.

- Verb traer- to bring

Yo	traigo	Nosotros	traemos
Tú	traes	Ustedes	traen
Ella/él/usted	trae	Ellos/ellas	traen

Notice that the "yo" form has a different spelling, but the rest of the conjugations follow the rules.

- Verb decir- to say

Yo	digo	Nosotros	decimos
Tú	dices	Ustedes	dicen
Ella/él/usted	dice	Ellos/ellas	dicen

If you could draw a boot around this verb chart, *nosotros* would be outside the boot.

Normally, when there are spelling changes to the root of the word, *nosotros* is left out of it.

The root of decir becomes 'dic' for most of this conjugation, but for *nosotros*, it reverts to 'dec.' You can see this same pattern in the chart below.

- Verb venir- to come

Yo	vengo	Nosotros	venimos
Tú	vienes	Ustedes	vienen
Ella/él/usted	viene	Ellos/ellas	vienen

Poner becomes pongo for "yo."
Hacer becomes hago for "yo."

LET'S PRACTICE!

Irregular Verb Practice

You know what these verbs mean, so let's do a little practice.

Select the verb with the meaning that would make sense with each sentence and conjugate the verb to match the person.

Your options for this first practice are only the irregular verbs- *ir, venir, traer, poner, hacer, tener,* and *decir.*

Mi padre _____ un pastel (a cake) para mi cumpleaños (birthday).
Mi amiga _____ dos mascotas, un perro y un gato.
Yo _____ un pastel en el horno (oven).
Ellos _____ las mochilas en la mesa.
Yo _____ "feliz cumpleaños".
Tú _____ a la tienda.
Yo _____ a estudiar a la noche (at night).
Yo _____ un libro para mi amigo.

Adverbs of Frequency

You could use many words to describe your actions, but we will focus on how often you do things in this section. Here is a list of adverbs that talk about frequency.

- Siempre- always
- Casi siempre- almost always
- Muchas veces/ regularmente- often
- A veces- sometimes
- Casi nunca- almost never
- Nunca- never

Using the present tense, you can discuss how often you do different actions. Read these example sentences.

- Yo siempre bebo café. I always drink coffee.
- Ellos casi nunca estudian. They almost never study.
- Yo como pizza regularmente. I often eat pizza.

If someone asked you how often you do something, they might ask one of these questions.

- ¿Con qué frecuencia limpias la casa? How often do you clean your house?
- ¿Cada cuánto comes fruta? How often do you eat fruit?

LET'S PRACTICE!

Try to answer the following questions with a full sentence.

¿Cada cuánto estudias español?

_____

¿Con qué frecuencia montas en bicicleta?

_____

¿Con qué frecuencia vas a la piscina?

_____

¿Cada cuánto bebes agua?

_____

Here are some sample answers to the above questions.

Yo estudio español a veces. - I sometimes study Spanish.
Yo nunca monto en bicicleta. - I never ride a bike.
Yo casi nunca voy a la piscina. - I almost never go to the pool.
Yo siempre bebo agua. - I always drink water.

You now have a solid vocabulary and know the basics behind making grammatically correct sentences. In the next chapter, you will work on adding some phrases to your vocabulary so that you can greet and start conversations with other people.

CHAPTER 8

GREETINGS AND INTRODUCTIONS

Make sure you spend time between each chapter practicing what you know. Even conversing with yourself can be a great way to practice your vocabulary. Reading as many sentences as possible will also help you become more comfortable speaking what you have written. Often, Spanish learners can write what they want to say but have trouble saying it. And this is also true for many people learning a new language. Make sure that you are comfortable writing what you want to say and saying it out loud.

Meetings and Greetings

Before practicing everything you have learned, review this list of greetings. With each list, the phrase's meaning and its literal translation will be included if they aren't the same. Sometimes, we want to say things exactly how we say them in English, but we must understand that the phrases are here to help you sound more like a native.

¡Hola!	Hello!
¡Buenos días!	Good morning!
¡Buenas tardes!	Good afternoon!
¡Buenas noches!	Good night!
¡Hasta pronto!	See you soon!
¡Hasta luego!	See you later!
¡Hasta mañana!	See you tomorrow!
Tengo que irme!	I have to go!
¡Nos vemos!	See you!
¡Adiós!	Goodbye!

Note that there is no *good evening,* so *buenas tardes* is used later in the day, than we would in English. Also, 'good night' is typically used as a goodbye in English. However, in Spanish, we can also use *Buenas noches* as a greeting.
Good night! How are you? Buenas noches, ¿cómo estás?

Question marks in Spanish

Do you notice that there is a ¿ at the beginning of questions in Spanish?

Since word order in Spanish doesn't change that much from a statement to a question, this emphasizes that a question is being asked from the beginning. If the question is a yes or no, then the phrasing is the same. The ¿ at the beginning of the sentence indicates right away that it's a question, not a statement.

For example-
Te gusta el helado- You like ice cream.
¿Te gusta el helado? - Do you like ice cream?

Asking how someone is doing

¿Cómo estás? And *¿Cómo está?* are the basic questions used to ask how someone is doing.

Based on what you know, do you know which ending is informal and which is formal?

Hint- look at the ending of *estás*. This version is for *tú,* so it's informal. If you want to ask someone you are meeting for the first time, you will use the more formal- *está.*

You can also ask-
- ¿Qué tal? - What's up?

This question is informal, something you would ask your friends or classmates.

Possible answers to the above questions are-
- Estoy bien- I'm fine/ good
- Estoy mal- I'm bad
- OR any other emotion words that you know- enojado, cansado, enfermo, etc.

If you're meeting someone for the first time, you might also ask
- ¿Cómo se llama? (formal) - ¿Cómo te llamas? (informal) What's your name? The literal translation is what do you call yourself?

You might answer-
- Me llamo _____o Mi nombre es

- ¿Y usted? ¿Y tú? - and you? This phrase would be used after someone has just answered a question and wants to turn the question back on you. For example, if you just ask someone's name. They might say- Me llamo Marcos. ¿Y usted? They could also be informal and say '¿Y tú?' The letter 'y' when standing on its own, is pronounced like ee and means and.

- ¿Cuántos años tienes? - How old are you?

- Tengo _____ años. - I am _____ years old. You also use the verb 'tener' (to have) in your answer.

Once you've asked someone's name and officially met them, you might use one of the following phrases.
- Mucho gusto- It's nice to meet you.
- Encantado/a- Nice to meet you.

Note that if you are a male, you will use the 'o' ending currently on the word *encantado*. If you're a female, you will change the ending to 'a.' *Encantada.*

To take leave of someone, you could use one of the following phrases.
- Adiós- Goodbye.
- Hasta luego- see you later
- Chao/Chau- pronounced like chow. It's an informal way of saying goodbye and is used more commonly in some countries than others.
- Cuídese (formal) Cuídate (informal) - Take care
- Que tenga/tengas un buen día- Have a good day

Here are a few polite phrases that you might have a chance to use.
- Gracias- thank you
- De nada- You're welcome. The literal meaning is *de-* of/from and *nada-* nothing, which means more like "it's nothing".
- Con gusto- My pleasure or with pleasure
- Disculpe (formal) / Disculpa (informal) - Excuse me. You use this more when trying to get someone's attention or start a conversation.
- Perdón/Disculpas- Excuse me or literally- pardon me. You would use this more when you've made a mistake and wish to ask forgiveness. For example, if you just said something incorrectly or stepped on someone's toe.
- Lo siento- I'm sorry. This phrase translates to "I feel it". You are sympathizing with the person's pain. Think of it like that when you use it.
- Por favor- Please or literally for my pleasure.

¿Cómo estás? (informal)	How are you?
¿Cómo está? (formal)	How are you?
Mucho gusto	It is nice to meet you
Encantado/a	Nice to meet you
Bienvenido/a	Welcome
Estoy bien	I am fine
Estoy muy cansado/a	I am very tired
Estoy mal	I am bad
No estoy bien	I am not OK
Estoy enfermo/a	I am sick
Estoy feliz	I am happy

¿Cómo te llamas? (informal)	What is your name?
¿Cómo se llama? (formal)	What is your name?
¿De dónde eres? (informal)	Where are you from?
¿De dónde es usted?(formal)	Where are you from?
Me llamo	My name is
Mi nombre es	My name is
¿Cuántos años tienes?	How old are you?
Tengo …..años	I am ……years old.
Soy de	I am from
Vivo en	I live in
¡Que tengas un buen día!	Have a good day!

¡Muchas gracias!	Thank you very much
Por favor	Please
¡De nada!	You are welcome!
¡Cuídate!	Take care!
Lo siento	I am sorry
Perdón/Disculpas	I am sorry
Con permiso	Excuse me

LET'S PRACTICE!

Practice these phrases by completing the conversation with someone you have just met. Write how you would respond to their sentence, then read the conversation aloud.

- Hola, buenos días.
- _____
- ¿Cómo está usted?
- _____
- Estoy bien, gracias.
- _____
- Me llamo José. ¿Y usted?
- _____
- Mucho gusto.
- _____

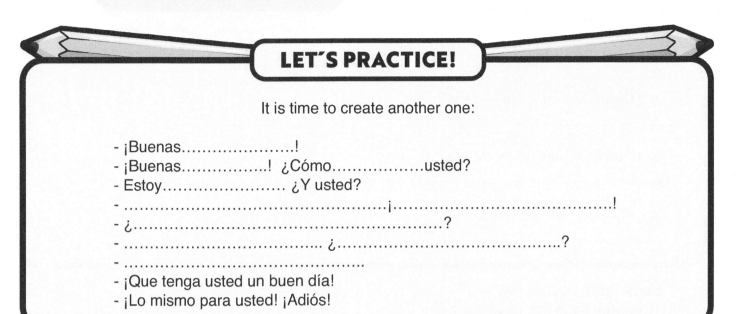

It is time to create another one:

- ¡Buenas......................!
- ¡Buenas................! ¿Cómo.................usted?
- Estoy........................ ¿Y usted?
- ....¡...!
- ¿...?
- .... ¿...?
- ....
- ¡Que tenga usted un buen día!
- ¡Lo mismo para usted! ¡Adiós!

Other Important Phrases for Spanish Learners

If you hear a phrase or word you don't understand, being able to ask what it means is important. Practice the following phrases by reading them out loud and memorizing them.

¿Cómo se dice _____ en español? - How do you say _____ in Spanish?
¿Puede repetir, por favor? - Can you repeat it, please? (formal)
¿Podrías repetir, por favor? - Could you repeat it please? (informal)
¿Qué significa _____? - What does _____ mean?
Más lento, por favor- Slower please.
No entiendo- I don't understand.
No sé- I don't know.

Practice, Practice, Practice

Below is a short paragraph.

First, please read through the paragraph out loud, focusing on using correct pronunciation.

Secondly, go through and find any words you don't understand and look them up.

Then, see if you can answer the questions about the passage.

Hola, me llamo Viviana. Tengo quince años. Vivo en Puerto Rico, pero soy de Colombia. Yo vivo en mi casa con mi madre y mi padre. También tengo cuatro mascotas: dos perros y dos gatos. Voy a la escuela y después, voy a la piscina con mis amigos.

1. ¿Cuántos años tiene Viviana?
_____

2. ¿Dónde (where) vive Viviana?
_____

3. ¿Qué edad tiene Viviana?
_____

Some hints/algunas pistas
1. Viviana tiene quince años.
2. Viviana vive en Puerto Rico.
3. Viviana tiene cuatro mascotas. (For this one, you might also have put that she has friends, which would be correct as well).

Note- '¿qué tiene?' can ask what she has if she's not feeling well. You might answer by saying "Tiene sueño" (she's tired). However, based on this little reading passage, talking about her friends or pets would make the most sense.

Your Turn

Create an introduction for yourself by answering the following questions. A sample introduction has been provided below the questions; you can use it to help format your answers.

- ¿Cómo te llamas?
- ¿Cuántos años tienes?
- ¿Dónde vives?
- ¿Cómo eres? Though this translates to "how are you", remember that eres, a version of ser, has been used, so it can't be asking about feelings. It asks for a literal description of your characteristics- gracioso, fuerte, alto, bajo, etc.
- ¿Tienes mascotas?

....
....
....
....
....
....
....

Extra Practice

Here is some extra practice so you don't forget what you've learned in previous chapters. Along with the instructions for each exercise, you can find the chapter you need to refer to if you are having trouble completing the exercise.

Pick between 'estar' and 'ser' and conjugate them
for each of the following sentences (Chapter 5).

- Ella _____ mi amiga.
- Nosotros _____ enojados.
- Yo _____ de los Estados Unidos.
- _____ las tres de la tarde.

-Choose between the options *el, la, los,* and *las* f
or each of the following sentences (Chapter 2).

- No tengo _____ libro de español.
- Ellos tienen _____ carros grandes.
- Él tiene _____ cama blanda.
- _____ camisas son amarillas.

Practice conjugating the following verbs to match each person.
Some of the verbs given are irregular (Chapter 7).

- Yo (practicar) _____
- Mis amigos (ir) _____
- Tú (decir) _____
- Nosotros (hablar) _____
- Ella (escribir) _____
- Yo (poner) _____

Take a moment to celebrate.
You've only gone through eight chapters and can speak some basic Spanish.

Constantly look for ways to expand your vocabulary. For example, try to name things or make sentences about them as you are doing them. If you are walking to your room, make a sentence. Yo camino a _____. If you don't know the word for room (it hasn't been in this book yet), then look it up!

CHAPTER 9

DAYS, DATES, AND TIMES

Days, Months, Seasons

Before discussing how to use the days of the week or months of the year, you first need to study the vocabulary. Also note that the first day of the week in Spanish is Monday, not Sunday. Calendars for Latino countries will also reflect this difference. Let´s review what we have learned in Chapter 2.

Días de la semana

Monday	lunes
Tuesday	martes
Wednesday	miércoles
Thursday	jueves
Friday	viernes
Saturday	sábado
Sunday	domingo
Weekend	fin de semana

Meses del año

January	enero
February	febrero
March	marzo
April	abril
May	mayo
June	junio
July	julio
August	agosto
September	septiembre
October	octubre
November	noviembre
December	diciembre

Estaciones del año

otoño	invierno	primavera	verano
Fall	Winter	Spring	Summer

Here are a few important notes about the days, months, and seasons.

Days, months, and seasons are not capitalized in Spanish. A holiday is called feriado. It is usually because of a special date in that country like Independence Day.

The days of the week in Spanish are masculine so we say: el lunes, el martes, el míercoles, el jueves, el viernes, el sábado, el domingo. We can talk about the days in plural, as los lunes, los martes, los miércoles, los jueves, los viernes, los sábados, los domingos.

We can abbreviate the Spanish days of the week using a single letter as: L, M, M, J, V, S, or D or a two-letter abbreviation to not get confused with martes and miércoles: Lu, Ma, Mi, Ju, Vi, Sa, Do.

We don't say ON a certain day in Spanish, like I will do this ON that day, we just say THE day. We use the masculine, singular form of the.

Take a look at these example sentences.

- Yo voy a la tienda **el l**unes.
- Ellos estudian para el examen **en j**unio.

They aren't capitalized, and I used *el lunes* instead of *en lunes*.
Here are a few more related words to what you are learning.

- El cumpleaños- the birthday
- Feriado- holiday
- Fecha- date
- Hoy- today
- Mañana- tomorrow (this same word also means morning)
- Ayer- yesterday

Telling the Date

Now that you have some new vocabulary, let's discuss how to use it. First, when telling the fecha, you start with the day and then the month.

For example, if you would write a date like 4/16/22 in English, you would flip the day and month to look like this in Spanish- 16/4/22.

You also change how you say it and ALWAYS start with the day.
- Hoy es dieciséis de abril.

Here are a few more examples; you can practice telling the date.

23/10	Hoy es veintitrés de octubre.
12/8	Hoy es doce de agosto.
6/9	Hoy es seis de septiembre.

¿Cuándo es tu cumpleaños?
Mi cumpleaños es el 15 de noviembre.

¿Cuándo es la independencia de los Estados Unidos?
La independencia de los Estados Unidos es…………………………………………
¿Cuándo es Noche de Brujas (Halloween)?
La Noche de Brujas es ……………………………………………………………

Notice the cardinal numbers are not changed to ordinal numbers-
i.e. sixteen to sixteenth or twenty-three to twenty-third.

You just use the regular number words (cardinal numbers) for dates
EXCEPT for the first of the month.

For the first, you use el primero, which means "the first". Here is an example-

- 1/10 Hoy es el primero de octubre.

Practice writing sentences to tell what today's date is.

a. 30/5 _____
b. 18/2 _____
c. 20/7 _____
d. 25/12 _____
e. 9/6 _____

Useful vocabulary

El día	The day
El fin de semana	The weekend
Ahora	Now
Este jueves	This Thursday
El próximo viernes	Next Friday
El viernes que viene	Next Friday
Pasado	Past
Pronto	Soon
Temprano	Early
Tarde	Late

Más temprano	Earlier
Más tarde	Later
Hasta el lunes	Until Monday
Antes del miércoles	Before Wednesday
Después del miércoles	After Wednesday
Desde el domingo	Since Sunday
Algunos días	Some days
Todo el día	All day
Todos los días	Everyday
Cada sábado	Every Saturday
El sábado	On Saturday
El sábado por la mañana	Saturday morning
Mañana por la tarde	Tomorrow afternoon
Mañana por la tarde	Tomorrow evening
Mañana por la noche	Tomorrow night
Pasado mañana	The day after tomorrow
En dos/tres/cuatro/etc. Días	In two/three/four/etc. days

Telling Time

A few chapters ago, you learned the basic phrase for telling time and how it uses the verb *ser*. Remember that if you are talking about one o'clock, we use the singular way and say the phrase *Es la*. We use the phrase Son las when talking about two o'clock or after.

Here are some other important phrases and vocabulary you will need to know to tell time.
- De la mañana- in the morning
- De la tarde- in the afternoon
- De la noche- in the night
- Y media- and half an hour or thirty minutes
- Y cuarto- and a quarter hour
- Y- past
- Menos- less or minus
- Medianoche- midnight
- Mediodía- midday

Note: In Spanish you can say *de la mañana* for the a.m. period and *de la noche* for the p.m. period. Another way to say this is using the 24-hour notation.

Let´s see these examples:
1. Son las tres de la mañana. (3:00 AM)
2. Son las cuatro y cuarto. (4:15hs)
3. Son las diez y media. (10:30hs)
4. Son las siete menos cuarto de la tarde. (6:45 PM)
5. Son las 9 y media de la noche. (9:30 PM)

LET´S PRACTICE!

Read these example sentences and try to figure out what time it is.
a. Son las cinco y media.   _____
b. Son las diez y cuarto.   _____
c. Son las doce menos cinco.   _____
d. Es la una y diez.   _____
e. Son las once y veinte.   _____
f. Son las ocho menos diez.   _____

The two trickiest ones are c. and f. because they use the word *menos*.
Remember that menos means "minus".

The first part says Son *las doce*, so what number is *doce*?
• Doce = twelve
So, this sentence is saying "it's twelve o'clock."

The second part says, *menos cinco*.
• Menos= minus
• Cinco = five
So what is twelve o'clock minus five minutes? 11:55.

Look at the last one again (f).
• Son las ocho- It's eight o'clock
• Menos diez- minus ten minutes.
• That makes it 7:50.

Let´s practice one more time! Connect with lines

Son las ocho y diez. •	• 7:15 hs
Son las diez menos diez. •	• 8:10hs
Son las tres menos veinte •	• 4:45 hs
Son las cuatro y veinte. •	• 9:50hs
Son las doce y veinticinco. •	• 2:40 hs
Son las ocho menos veinticinco •	• 12:25 hs
Son las cinco menos cuarto •	• 4:20 hs
Son las siete y cuarto •	• 7:35hs

Those are the basics to telling time, though you can always be more specific and say what part of the day. For example,
- Son las once de la mañana. It's eleven in the morning.
- Son las cuatro de la tarde. It's four in the afternoon.

LET'S PRACTICE!

Practice writing the following times out in full sentences.
Remember to start with *Es la* or *Son las*.

4:30	_____
10:20	_____
7:15	_____
8:55	_____

Now, if you are telling AT what time something will be, you wouldn't use the *Son las* or *Es la* phrases, because those identify the current time. You would use the phrase *a las* or *a la*. In this case, *a* stands for "at". Read these examples.

- Yo tengo una clase a las cuatro. I have a class at four o'clock.
- Ellos van a la escuela a las nueve de la mañana. They go to school at nine in the morning.

If you want to ask questions about the time, you will use these questions- ¿Qué hora es? (What time is it?) '
¿A qué hora…? (At what time…?)

Let's practice! Can you read out loud?

- ¿A qué hora es la clase de danzas?
- La clase de danzas es a las 3 de la tarde.

- Disculpe, señor, ¿qué hora es?
- Son las 8:30 hs

- ¿A qué hora tienes cita con el médico?
- Mi cita con el médico es a las cuatro y cuarto.

Choose the correct time:

4:00hs
- Son las cuatro.
- Son las ocho.

11:40hs
- Son las once y veinte
- Son las doce menos veinte

9:40hs
- Son las diez menos veinte
- Son las nueve y veinte

9:50hs
- Son las diez menos cuarto
- Son las diez menos diez

5:10hs
- Son las cuatro y diez
- Son las cinco y diez

3:20hs
- Son las tres y veinte
- Son las tres menos veinte

2:45hs
- Son las tres menos cuarto
- Son las dos y cuarto

7:15hs
- Son las siete menos cuarto
- Son las siete y cuarto

Answer the following questions using the vocabulary and information you have learned in this chapter.

- ¿Qué hora es? _____
- ¿A qué hora tienes clase de español? _____
- ¿A qué hora es la película del cine? _____
- ¿A qué hora es el programa de TV? _____
- ¿A qué hora desayunas? _____

Write the following times in full sentences.

- 2:30 _____
- 12:10 _____
- 4:15 _____
- 10:55 _____

Putting It All Together

Here is a good chance to review not only what you've learned today, but what you have learned throughout these nine chapters. If you find yourself struggling with a certain area, it might be time to go back and do a little review of the specific chapter.

Complete this dialogue.

- ¡Hola! ¡Buenas tardes!..Pedro
- ¡Buenas tardes, Pedro! Soy …………………………... ¿ usted?
- Estoy   ¡   ! ¿ _?
- Yo soy de   ¿ y usted?
- Yo soy de …………………............ pero vivo en …………………………………
- ¡Un gusto en conocerlo!¡Adiós!
- ¡Hasta pronto!

¿La, el, las o los?

	casa		perro		mesa
	carpeta		cepillos		cuchara
	regalo		manzana		tortugas
	planta		sillas		vaso
	candados		caballo		gatas

Choose an adjective for each noun

tío		perro		comida	
lavadora		pantalón		pelota	
camión		elefante		libro	

Choose a noun for each adjective

	pesado		comunicativo		sucio
	liviano		frío		triste
	caliente		inquieto		limpia

Complete the tables

Five feminine nouns	Five masculine adjectives

Five singular words	Five plural words

Complete the sentences with the proper colors

Los colores de la bandera de los Estados Unidos son
....
La lechuga es ....
El chocolate es ....
Y el café es ....
Me gustan las fresas ....

Which days or months are missing?

lunes			jueves	
	viernes			lunes
		octubre		
	domingo			
junio				
		febrero		abril

Complete the sentences using the correct verbs.

Yo (tener) ………………..diez años.
Los padres (vivir) …………………………………………….en los Estados Unidos.
Nosotros (caminar) ……………………………………..por la playa todos los días.
Mi cumpleaños (ser) ………………..el miércoles 8 de febrero.
María (cocinar) ……………………………………..un rico pastel de chocolate.
Usted siempre (comer)…………………………………..verduras.
Ellos (estar) ……………………………………………..en reunión de trabajo ahora.
Mi hermano (vender) ………………………………………..su bicicleta azul.
Mariano (escribir) ………………………………….para un periódico de noticias.
María y José (comprar) ……………………………………pan y hamburguesas.

One more quick chance to review. Let's make sure you remember all
of those verb endings. Change the verb to match the person.

Yo (enseñar) _____
Nosotros (comer) _____
Él (beber) _____
Tú (manejar) _____
Mis amigos (ir) _____
Yo (ir) _____
Usted (poner) _____
Yo (tener) _____

One more topic: Reflexive Verbs

Reflexive verbs are those whose subject and object are the same, for example: I look at myself. *Yo me miro*. A reflexive pronoun can be used because it shows that the subject acts upon itself and differs for each person. Examples of conjugated reflexive verbs are:

Yo **me** miro
Tú **te** miras
Él/ella/usted **se** mira
Nosotros **nos** miramos
Ellos/Ellas/ Ustedes **se** miran

The reflexive pronoun is always before the conjugated verb form and can be joined to the end of an infinitive verb. These are examples of some reflexive verbs in Spanish:

- Despertarse- to wake up
- Levantarse- to get up
- Cepillarse los dientes- to brush your teeth
- Ducharse- to have a shower
- Bañarse- to have a bath
- Vestirse- to get dressed
- Peinarse- to comb
- Maquillarse- to makeup
- Afeitarse- to shave
- Irse- to leave
- Acostarse- to go to bed
- Sentarse- to sit
- Dormirse- to go to sleep

Read the following routine and then write one about yourself. Practice dates and times as you write it.

De lunes a viernes me levanto a las siete en punto. Siempre me despierto antes de que suene el despertador. Me cepillo los dientes y me peino. Luego, me gusta desayunar. Después, me ducho rápido y me visto todavía más rápido. Me maquillo en diez minutos y me voy al trabajo. A la salida del trabajo, hago compras y luego preparo la cena. Me siento un rato a leer algún libro y me acuesto cerca de las diez. Me duermo muy rápido porque estoy cansada. Los fines de semana me levanto cerca de las diez. Me voy a desayunar a algún café y por la tarde organizo algún plan con amigos. Los sábados me acuesto muy tarde.

Highlight the reflexive verbs in the text and write one of your own. Here is the translation:

From Monday to Friday, I get up at seven o'clock. I'm always awake before the alarm clock rings. I brush my teeth and do my hair. Then I like to have breakfast. After that, I take a quick shower and get dressed even faster. I do my make-up in ten minutes and leave for work. After work, I do some shopping and then I prepare dinner. I sit to read a book for a while and go to bed around ten. I fall asleep immediately because I'm really tired. At weekends, I get up around ten. I go to a cafe to have breakfast and plan to do something with my friends in the afternoon. On Saturdays, I go to bed late.

CHAPTER 10

ASKING QUESTIONS

Many meetings between people begin with questions and answers. How are you? What's your name? Where are you from? What do you do? You already know how to ask some of the most basic questions, but in this chapter, you will learn the question words and how to form questions on your own, rather than just memorizing the questions you are most likely to ask. Let's get started!

Yes/No Questions

Let's start with something easy. Yes or no questions are said the same way you would say the statement. For example, if I want to say "Do you drink?" (you drink)

Besides the tone of voice to ask a question, the Yes and No questions are easy to ask and spot in writing. In the case of a written question, you will notice question marks at the beginning and end of the sentence.

- ¿Tú bebes? - question
- Tú bebes- statement

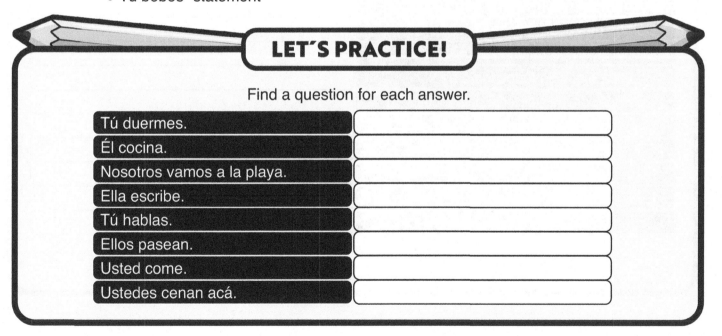

LET´S PRACTICE!

Find a question for each answer.

Tú duermes.	
Él cocina.	
Nosotros vamos a la playa.	
Ella escribe.	
Tú hablas.	
Ellos pasean.	
Usted come.	
Ustedes cenan acá.	

If you answer a question negatively, you often want to use two 'no's.'
Look at this example

- ¿Tú bebes? - question- Do you drink?
- No, no bebo. - answer- No, I don't.

Note that the person who answers the question is different, then the pronoun changes too. Let's practice! Find a negative answer for each question. Connect with lines.

¿Compras un poco de queso? •	• No, nosotros no bailamos tango.
¿Lees las noticias todos los días? •	• No, no limpio mi dormitorio.
¿Quieres beber un jugo de naranja? •	• No, no quiero beber un jugo de naranja.
¿Bailan tango ustedes? •	• No, no juego mucho al golf.
¿Limpias tu dormitorio? •	• No, no compro un poco de queso.
¿Juegas mucho al golf? •	• No, mis manos no están sucias.
¿Es un día soleado? •	• No, no leo las noticias todos los días
¿Están sucias tus manos? •	• No, no es un día soleado.

Answer these questions by yourself using a negative form as an example.

¿Traen ustedes un regalo?	No, nosotros no traemos un regalo.
¿Cantan ustedes una canción?	
¿Juega tenis?	
¿Comes pastel de manzanas?	
¿Compras un pantalón azul?	
¿Practica ejercicio todos los días?	
¿Tenemos comida suficiente para todos?	
¿Estudias a la mañana o a la noche?	
¿Comes mucha pizza?	
¿Manejas un carro?	
¿Estudias para el examen?	
¿Ordenamos un poco esta casa?	

Question Words

Like in English, you need to know a list of question words to ask more complex questions. Spend time getting to know these words and try to think of a question or two you could ask with each one.

- Dónde- where
- Adónde- where… to
- Cuándo- when
- Quién- who
- Qué- what
- Por qué- why
- Para qué- why (In English it would be "what are you doing this for")
- Cómo- how
- Cuánto- how many or how much (this question word can change forms to be *cuánta, cuántos,* or *cuántas* if you're asking about feminine or plural things)
- Cada cuánto – how often

You can use the phrase *¿Cada cuánto?* or *¿Con qué frecuencia?* Neither of these question phrases uses the word cómo, even though *cómo* translates to how.

Let's review some sample questions you might hear when talking to someone.

¿Quién eres?	Who are you?
¿Quién es tu maestra?	Who is your teacher?
¿Quién es tu madre?	Who is your mother?
¿Quiénes son ellos?	Who are they?
¿De dónde eres?	Where are you from?
¿Dónde estás?	Where are you?
¿Dónde está tu cuaderno?	Where is your notebook?
¿Dónde vives?	Where do you live?
¿Qué es aquel edificio?	What is that building?
¿Cómo preparas un pastel?	How do you prepare a cake?
¿Cuántos años tienes?	How old are you?
¿Cuántas mascotas tienes?	How many pets do you have?
¿Cuántos hermanos tienes?	How many siblings do you have?
¿Cuándo es la clase?	When is the class?
¿Cuándo es tu vuelo?	When is your flight?
¿Cuándo es el examen?	When is the test?
¿Cómo es tu hermano?	How is your brother?
¿Qué necesitas?	What do you need?
¿Qué es eso?	What is that?
¿Qué comes?	What do you eat?
¿Por qué te gusta el pan?	Why do you like bread?
¿Cada cuánto pasa el tren?	How often does the train pass by?
¿Por qué estás aquí?	Why are you here?
¿Por qué estudias español?	Why do you study Spanish?

Read aloud these answers and questions.

¿Cómo eres?	Yo soy artística y perezosa.
¿Qué es esto?	Esto es un lápiz.
¿Cuándo es la clase?	La clase es el lunes.
¿Cada cuánto estudias?	Estudio a veces.
¿Qué día es hoy?	Hoy es jueves.
¿Dónde está tu madre?	Mi madre está en la cocina.
¿Dónde estudias?	Estudio en la biblioteca.
¿Tienes un lápiz?	Sí, tengo un lápiz.

LET'S PRACTICE!

Now answer the following questions by yourself.

• ¿Cómo se llama la película?
_____

• ¿Dónde están tus zapatos?
_____

• ¿Cuál es el número de teléfono de aquí?
_____

• ¿Quién es Tomás?
_____

• ¿Qué día es tu cumpleaños?
_____

• ¿Cuántas pizzas ordeno?
_____

• ¿Qué traes en tu mochila?
_____

• ¿Cuántos libros tienes en la mesa?
_____

The more you practice creating, thinking, and saying your answers out loud and writing them, the more comfortable you will feel.

Questions with prepositions

Some questions in English end with prepositions. For example,

- Who are you speaking to?
- Where are you from?
- What car are you interested in?
- What are you angry about?

These examples end with a word that is part of a prepositional phrase. In Spanish, we place the preposition at the beginning of the question.

What did you call me for?	¿Para qué me has llamado?
What are you talking about?	¿De qué estás hablando?
Which country are you flying to?	¿A qué país estás viajando?
Who is the present for?	¿Para quién es el regalo?
What are these things for?	¿Para qué son estas cosas?
Who would you like to go with?	¿Con quién te gustaría ir?
What are you both playing at?	¿A qué están jugando ustedes dos?
Where do you come from?	¿De dónde vienes?

While talking about prepositions, let's go over a list of the most common prepositions in Spanish.

- A- to
- De- of/from
- Para- for, by
- Por- also for (we can get into the differences between the two of these later)
- Sobre- about
- En- in/on
- Con- with
- Desde- Since/from

Let's look at the above questions in Spanish.

- ¿Con quién estás hablando? With whom are you speaking?
- ¿En qué carro estás interesado? What car are you interested in?
- ¿De dónde eres? Where are you from?
- ¿Adónde vas? Where are you going? (Note that the preposition is attached to the word *dónde*)

You may need to think of the whole question you want to ask, think about if you need to move any of the words so that the placement is correct in Spanish, *then* ask it in Spanish.

LET'S PRACTICE!

Ask the following questions in Spanish.

Where are you going?	
Which school do you go to?	
Whom are you going with?	
Who are you cooking with?	
Who is this shirt for?	
What is this book about?	

There is, There are

There is and there are, are expressed in Spanish using "hay," a form of the verb haber (to have). "Hay" refers to existence. So, we can ask and answer questions using this word. Here there are some examples:

¿Hay mesas en la fiesta?	Are there tables at the party?
¿Hay suficientes manzanas?	Are there enough apples?
Hay muchas personas aquí.	There are many people here.
Hay una abeja en mi sopa.	There is a bee in my soup.
¿Hay una escalera para subir?	Is there a ladder to go up?
Hay niños en el parque.	There are children at the park.
Hay regalos para todos.	There are presents for everybody.
Hay un perfume agradable a flores.	There is a nice floral perfume.

LET'S PRACTICE!

Create sentences to give the following information.

- There is a bed in the bedroom. _____

- There are children at the park. _____

- There is a lot of fruit. _____

- There is water on the table. _____

As you can see, there are a lot of sentences and phrases you can make with this word. Remember that because of our pronunciation rules, it's not pronounced like *hay* that a horse would eat, but like *ayyyy* (think of a pirate).

Practice

Create ten questions you might want to ask if you are just meeting someone for the first time. Here is a list of some common ones below. See if you can add to it.

¿Dónde trabajas?	Where do you work?
¿Dónde hay buena comida?	Where is there good food?
¿Cómo es la comida aquí?	How is the food here?
¿Qué lugares debo visitar?	Where should I visit?
¿Cómo puedo llegar allí?	How can I get there?
¿Cuánto cuesta un boleto?	How much does a ticket cost?

Many businesses focused on tourism may have websites with information, but many smaller restaurants and family-owned businesses won't have information online. The best way to learn about them and visit the hidden gems is by asking people who live there.

CHAPTER 11

GETTING ABOUT

In Chapter 2 we learned about asking for directions with simple words or sentences such as:

Disculpas, ¿dónde hay un supermercado?	Excuse me, where is a supermarket?
¿Hay un hospital por aquí?	Is there a hospital near here?
A la izquierda	To the left
A la derecha	To the right
Atrás	Behind
Cerca	Near
Lejos	Far
En frente	In front

Direction Vocabulary

We will add a list of important vocabulary you need to know when asking questions. After working with them, we will discuss how to put them together to make sentences and questions.

El hotel	The hotel	El autobus	The bus
La casa	The house	El tren	The train
El apartamento	The apartment	La farmacia	The pharmacy
El edificio	The building	El centro comercial	The mall
La librería	The bookstore	El gimnasio	The gym
La gasolinería	The gas station	El parque	The park
El consultorio médico	The doctor's office	El consultorio dental	The dentist's office
La carretera	The highway	La calle	The street
El estacionamiento	The parking lot	El puente	The bridge
El museo	The museum	Derecho	Straight
La biblioteca	The library	Al lado de	Beside
El hospital	The hospital	Entre	Between
La iglesia	The church	Doblar	To turn
El parque	The park	Seguir	To keep going
La parada del autobus	The bus stop	Tomar	To take
El supermercado	The supermarket	El semáforo	The traffic light
La estación de …	The … station	Próximo	Next

This may seem like a lot of vocabulary, but some words that describe places are similar to their English words.

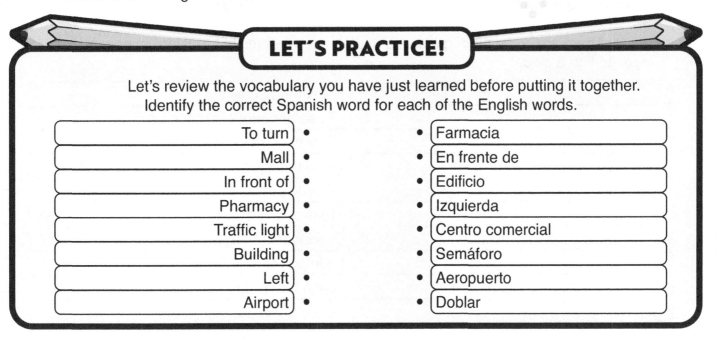

LET'S PRACTICE!

Let's review the vocabulary you have just learned before putting it together. Identify the correct Spanish word for each of the English words.

To turn •	• Farmacia
Mall •	• En frente de
In front of •	• Edificio
Pharmacy •	• Izquierda
Traffic light •	• Centro comercial
Building •	• Semáforo
Left •	• Aeropuerto
Airport •	• Doblar

Asking for Directions

There are several ways to ask for directions. The easiest one is just saying the name of the place you are looking for using the correct intonation as a question. It could sound as:

- Disculpe, ¿la farmacia?
- Buenas tardes, ¿un hospital?
- Buenas noches, ¿el Bar Coyote?
- Disculpa, ¿la tienda de mascotas?

You can also tell someone that you are looking for a certain place and the other person will understand that you are looking for help and expect to receive directions. It could sound as:

- Estoy buscando un supermercado. (I am looking for a supermarket)
- Necesito un hospital. (I need a hospital)
- Busco el Museo de Arte. (I am looking for the Art Museum).

You can also ask for directions using complete sentences as:

- ¿Dónde está el hospital?
- ¿Dónde está el restaurante de María?
- ¿Dónde está el aeropuerto?
- ¿Dónde está el ascensor?
- ¿Cómo llego a la parada de autobús?
- ¿Cómo voy al puerto?
- ¿Hay un hotel por aquí?
- ¿Sabes si por aquí hay una tienda de café?

Remember that if someone starts answering you, and they speak too quickly, you can use the phrase *Más lento, por favor* to ask them to slow down.

There are some other questions and phrases that might be useful when you need to find a place:

I am lost.	Estoy perdido/a
Does the bus #86 pass by here?	¿Pasa por aquí el autobus 86?
Which is the best way to go to the port?	¿Cuál es el mejor camino para ir al puerto?
How far is the Science Museum?	¿Qué tan lejos es el Museo de Ciencias?
Where can I rent a bike?	¿Dónde puedo alquilar una bicicleta?
Is it far from here?	¿Está lejos de aquí?
Thank you for your help.	Gracias por su ayuda.
It is impossible to get lost.	Es imposible perderse.
I have another question.	Tengo otra pregunta.
I need help.	Necesito ayuda.

When asking for directions, you will need to ask clear questions. Read these example questions out loud.

- ¿Dónde está el hospital?
- ¿Dónde está el restaurante Maria's?
- ¿Dónde está el aeropuerto?

Cultural Note- While we are talking about directions, be aware that there are not a lot of street names in Latin America, or at least street names that are commonly used. If you are in the center of a city, you will easily be able to find the signs that tell you what street you are on, but leaving the main center area will be harder. This is why asking for directions will become very helpful.

Practice reading these sample instructions and figure out what you need to do.

1. *Camina derecho unos cinco minutos, luego dobla a la derecha en frente de Pops. La farmacia estará a tu derecha.*

This is written exactly like someone would give you directions, perhaps using a couple of words you don't know. That's okay. Skip over the words you don't know and focus on the ones you do. Also, many people will give directions and reference different stores or places to turn. Because street names aren't very common, people won't know their names or numbers by heart.

1. The first sentence uses the words *camina, derecho, cinco minutos*. These phrases mean "walk, straight, five minutes".
   You may not know all the connecting words, but you need to walk down the street for about five minutes in the direction the speaker is pointing.

2. Let's look at the second part of that sentence. Here are the words you might recognize- *dobla, derecha, en frente de* . . . which translate as "turn right, in front of . . . in front of what? Pops." This is the name of an ice cream chain store. Even if you don't know that, you can at least be on the lookout for stores named that.

3. The last sentence says a tu *derecha.* Do you recognize *derecha* as meaning right? The verb *estará* sounds like *estar,* which means "to be". So, it's saying something like 'it is on your right' or 'it will be on your right'. You can focus on the fact that you should look to the right after you make that turn.

It's okay to ask for directions more than once. Just like in the United States, people from different parts of different countries will have different accents. Some may be harder to understand than others. Some may speak faster or use vocabulary with which you are more familiar.

Practice figuring out the directions below.

1. *Camina derecho por diez minutos. Puedes doblar a la izquierda en la tienda con la vaca en frente. Después, dobla a la derecha en el consultorio. La farmacia está allí.*

Remember to focus on the words you know. You'll be okay without knowing every word. Here's a translation of the words you may recognize. Then, a more thorough translation is given below.

- Walk straight. . . ten minutes. . . . turn to the left at the store with the . . . in front. Afterward, turn to the right at the doctor's or dentist's office. The pharmacy is there.

You know most of the words, but here it is with the blanks filled in.

- Go straight for ten minutes. You can turn left at the store with the cow in front. Afterward, turn right at the doctor's/dentist's office. The pharmacy is there.

2. *Toma el bus cuarenta y siete hasta la escuela. Baja del bus y camina dos minutos. Allí está el hotel.*

- Take bus 47 . . . . school. . . .bus and walk two minutes. The hotel is there. Once again, here is the translation with the blanks filled in.
- Take bus 47 to the school. Get off the bus and walk for two minutes. The hotel is there.

3. *Necesitas seguir directo por dos cuadras. En la segunda calle, dobla a la derecha. Camina dos cuadras más y verás el gimnasio.*

- You need to keep straight for two . . . At the second street, turn right. Walk two . . . . and . . . the gym.

- You need to keep straight for two blocks. At the second street, turn right. Walk two blocks, and you will see the gym.

Necesitar - Deber - Tener que - Poder

These are useful verbs for expressing need, duty, ability, or possibility. You just saw many of them in the previous vocabulary and you will probably hear them when asking for directions. Let's see what they mean and how they all work.

- Necesito llegar a la estación de trenes. - I need to get to the train station.
- Debemos tomar el metro y luego caminar 5 cuadras. - We must take the metro and then walk 5 blocks.
- Tienes que caminar derecho y doblar a la izquierda. - You have to go straight and turn left.
- Puedes llegar al museo caminando desde aquí.- You can get to the museum by walking from here.

What do you notice about all these verbs? As in English, they are all used followed by a non-conjugated verb. Notice, however, that the verb *tener* uses *que* before the non-conjugated verb.

Remember that *tener (to have to)* is an irregular verb. And so is *poder (can)*. Here are their conjugations:

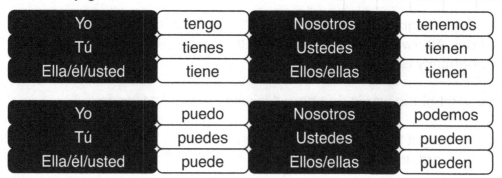

Yo	tengo	Nosotros	tenemos
Tú	tienes	Ustedes	tienen
Ella/él/usted	tiene	Ellos/ellas	tienen

Yo	puedo	Nosotros	podemos
Tú	puedes	Ustedes	pueden
Ella/él/usted	puede	Ellos/ellas	pueden

LET'S PRACTICE!

Try to answer these questions in Spanish using
the previous verbs and the vocabulary from this lesson.

¿Cómo puedo llegar al aeropuerto?

_____

¿Adónde tienes que ir?

_____

¿Dónde hay una farmacia?

_____

Estoy perdido. ¿Sabes dónde está la catedral?

_____

¿Cuántas cuadras debo caminar para llegar al Museo de Arte Moderno?

_____

Necesito ir a la estación de trenes. ¿Puedo caminar desde aquí?

_____

CHAPTER 12

ME GUSTA

Probably "gustar" is one of the most common verbs in Spanish and we will learn how to use it in this chapter. If you want to express liking something in English, you'd say for example- *I like chocolate*. You'd say- Me gusta el chocolate when expressing this idea in Spanish. Gustar means "to like". It is a pronominal or reflexive verb. The pronominal or reflexive verbs are refer to an action the subject carries out on himself. They are always conjugated with a reflexive pronoun that agrees with the number and person of the subject.

Also pay attention to the definite article *el* that should always be used in Spanish.

Me gusta el café.
Me gusta el color rojo.
Me gusta esa pelota verde.
Me gusta el agua fría.
Me gusta el teatro.

Look at this example- *Me gustan las películas españolas* "I like Spanish movies". Since what you like is plural (*las películas españolas*), the verb must be plural too (*gustan*).

Me gustan las manzanas deliciosas.
Me gustan los pasteles de chocolate.
Me gustan los libros de misterio.
Me gustan las películas de terror.
Me gustan los deportes peligrosos.

Gustar can also be combined with other verbs in the infinitive form. In this case, we always use the singular form.

Me gusta nadar.
Me gusta cantar.
Me gusta jugar tenis.
Me gusta montar a caballo.

And what do you notice about the person? There's no *yo* in these sentences, although they are translated as "I like" in English. So, this is the second important thing you need to remember when using the verb *gustar*. The Spanish subject of the sentence is the object or the action, which is why it needs an indirect object pronoun that changes according to the person who likes the object or the action. You should always use the following pronouns:

Yo	Yo
Yo	me
Tú	te
Él - Ella - Usted	le
Nosotros	nos
Ustedes	les
Ellos - Ellas	les

Here are some examples:

Nos gusta la pizza estilo Chicago. - We like Chicago style pizza.
Me gustan los libros de ciencia ficción. - I like science fiction books.
¿Te gusta el verano? - Do you like summer?

LET'S PRACTICE!

Connect with lines to create the correct sentences.

Me gusta •	• las hamburguesas con mayonesa
Nos gusta •	• leer libros de aventuras
Le gusta •	• jugar ajedrez
Les gusta •	• los deportes de riesgo
Me gustan •	• practicar baloncesto
Nos gustan •	• comer helado de chocolate
Te gusta •	• las fiestas en la playa
Les gustan •	• la comida china

Now, it is time to write your own sentences:

Me gusta ……………………………………………………………………
Les gusta ……………………………………………………………………
Te gustan ……………………………………………………………………

If you want to emphasize or clarify the person who likes something, you may use the preposition *a* with the name, the person or the first pronouns (except for *yo* and *tú*, see below), for example:

A ustedes les gusta el café italiano. - You like Italian coffee.
A mis amigos les gustan los días de lluvia. - My friends like rainy days.
A Julián le gustan los sándwiches de queso y tomate. - Julian likes cheese and tomato sandwiches.
A **mí** me gusta este artista. - I like this artist.
A **ti** te gusta el tenis. - You like tennis.

LET´S PRACTICE!

Let´s continue with your own sentences.

A mi mamá le gusta ....
A mí me gusta ....
A tus hijos les gusta ....
A esas mujeres les gusta ....

If you want to talk about dislikes, then you should place *no* before the pronoun:

No me gusta esta canción.- I don't like this song.
No me gusta el café frío. I do not like cold coffee.
No me gustan los días lluviosos. I do not like rainy days.

Answer the following questions.

¿Te gustan las películas de terror? Do you like horror films?
....

¿Te gusta el café con azúcar? Do you like coffee with sugar?
....

¿Te gustan los museos de arte moderno? Do you like modern art museums?
....

¿Te gusta el calor o el frío? Do you like hot or cold weather?
....

¿Te gusta el mar o te gustan las montañas? Do you like the sea or the mountains?
....

¿Te gusta o no te gusta? Complete these sentences.

.... montar a caballo.
....tocar la guitarra.
....beber leche caliente.
....leer un libro de amor.
....comer arroz con chocolate.
.... trabajar en un parque de diversiones.
.... tocar arañas con las manos.

Based on the following people´s personalities,
write two sentences expressing likes and dislikes. You can follow the example below.

Eres una persona deportista. (libros/entrenamientos)

• No te gusta leer libros.
• Te gusta hacer entrenamientos al aire libre.

Mis hermanos Tomás y Martín son atléticos. (bailar/practicar deportes)

•
•

Soy muy romántica. (películas de amor/películas de guerras)

•
•

Teresa tiene muchos amigos. (fiestas/caminar sola)

•
•

Likes and Dislikes

Gustar is not the only verb that works this way.
Many other verbs use the same structure. Let's see some of them.

encantar- to love
interesar- to interest
molestar- to bother
fastidiar- to annoy
aburrir- to bore
entusiasmar- to get excited about

Express your opinion about these topics using the previous verbs.

La gente soberbia. - The arrogant people
Las películas de acción. - Action movies
El tráfico. - The traffic
El humo del cigarrillo. - The cigarette smoke
La historia estadounidense. - American History
Los viajes al extranjero. - Traveling abroad
Las mentiras. - The lies
La comida asiática. - Asian food

....
....
....
....
....
....
....
....
....
....
....

LET'S PRACTICE!

Now, tell somebody else's opinion about the previous topics. Remember to change the pronoun! For example, *A mi hermano le encantan las películas de acción.*

....
....
....
....
....
....
....
....
....
....
....

Write a sentence using the following elements.

yo / encantar / estudiar español
Me encanta estudiar español.
....

él / molestar / viajar en metro
....

nosotros / gustar / caminar por la ciudad
....

ellos / aburrir / escuchar al profesor
....

ustedes / entusiasmar / conocer un nuevo país
....

yo / interesar / leer ficción
....

CHAPTER 13

SIMPLE PAST TENSE

In Spanish, we use five different tenses to speak about past actions. The most common tense used is the Simple Past Tense which describes actions that happened and concluded in the past. It is called the pretérito perfecto simple or pretérito indefinido and it is formed by only one word (the conjugated verb) without any auxiliary verb. The past tense will allow you to talk more about things you have done with your friends. The most important thing to remember when learning past tense is that just like present tense, there is a different ending for each person or group. However, many verbs will follow the same pattern once you learn the basic ending

Verbs

Before we get into the past tense endings, let's add a few more verbs to your vocabulary list. You already have a lot from chapter four, but you can always add more. Some of these are irregular in the present, which is noted if it's the case.

- Buscar- to look for
- Nacer- to be born
- Empezar- to begin
- Llegar- to arrive
- Llevar- to wear or to bring
- Dejar- to leave
- Llamar- to call
- Creer- to believe
- Volver- to return (irregular in present tense)
- Esperar- to hope for or to wait for
- Entender- to understand (irregular in present tense)
- Recordar- to remember (irregular in present tense)
- Pagar- to pay
- Cambiar- to change
- Ganar- to win or to earn

Past tense endings of regular verbs

As we have studied before, the verbs are split into three groups according to their infinitive endings: -ar, -er, and -ir. Each of these groups has slightly different conjugations. Let's look at just the endings here. Remember to remove the -ar, -er, -ir before adding new ending.

English	Pronoun	Ser		Estar	
I am	Yo	soy	(sohee)	estoy	(ehs-toy)
You are	Tú	eres	(eh-rehs)	estás	(ehs-tahs)
He/she has	Él/ella/usted	es	(ehs)	está	(ehs-tah)
We are	Nosotros/as	somos	(soh-mohs)	estamos	(ehs-tah-mohs)
You are	Vosotros/as	sois	(soh-is)	estáis	(ehs-tahis)
They are	Ellos/ellas/ustedes	son	sohn	están	(ehs-than)

Similar to the conjugation of the present tense, the changes are just in the ENDINGS. To form the new conjugation, you need to remove the *-ar* ending and replace it with the ending that matches your pronoun. Let's look at an example with *hablar*.

Yo	habl**é**	Nosotros	habl**amos**
Tú	habl**aste**	Ustedes	habl**aron**
Ella/él/usted	habl**ó**	Ellos/ellas	habl**aron**

Do you notice any endings that look familiar?

With *-ar* verbs, the *nosotros* ending is the same. For example, *estudiamos* can mean we are studying right now, or we studied before. You can tell the difference with contextual clues. For example, if the sentence says, *Nosotros estudiamos* ayer, then we know it's past tense since ayer means yesterday.

Please pay attention to the tilde over top of that *-o*. The tilde means that you stress that last syllable more when speaking it out loud, and you write it when writing the words so it's easier to tell if I am doing something now or if he or she did something before. Look here.

- Yo llamo a mi amigo. I call my friend.
- Él llamó a su amigo. He called his friend.

LET'S PRACTICE!

Let's practice with the verb trabajar (to work)

Yo		Nosotros	
Tú		Ustedes	
Ella/él/usted		Ellos/ellas	

Note: -ar verbs ending in -car, -gar, -zar have a change for the *yo* forms. Look at the following examples:

- Sacar- Yo saqué
- Pagar- Yo pagué
- Empezar- Yo empecé

-ER and -IR Verbs

Now, let's review the endings for *-er* and *-ir* verbs. They are the same for the past tense no matter if the verb originally ended with *-er* or *-ir*.

Verbo comer (to eat)

Yo	comí	Nosotros	comimos
Tú	comiste	Ustedes	comieron
Ella/él/usted	comió	Ellos/ellas	comieron

Verbo beber (to drink)

Yo	bebí	Nosotros	bebimos
Tú	bebiste	Ustedes	bebieron
Ella/él/usted	bebió	Ellos/ellas	bebieron

Verbo escribir (to write)

Yo	escribí	Nosotros	escribimos
Tú	escribiste	Ustedes	escribieron
Ella/él/usted	escribió	Ellos/ellas	escribieron

Verbo vivir (to live)

Yo	viví	Nosotros	vivimos
Tú	viviste	Ustedes	vivieron
Ella/él/usted	vivió	Ellos/ellas	vivieron

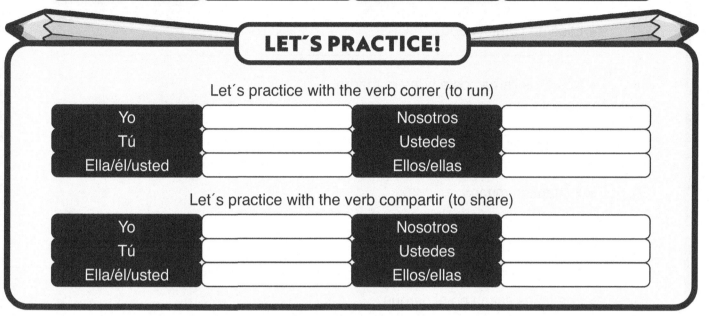

LET´S PRACTICE!

Let´s practice with the verb correr (to run)

Yo		Nosotros	
Tú		Ustedes	
Ella/él/usted		Ellos/ellas	

Let´s practice with the verb compartir (to share)

Yo		Nosotros	
Tú		Ustedes	
Ella/él/usted		Ellos/ellas	

One strange thing about the past tense with -er, -ir verbs is that the verb root ends with a vowel.

For example, leer ends with a vowel once we take off the end. We are just left with 'le'. That means for ella/ él/ usted and the ellos/ ustedes conjugation, we need to add 'yo' and 'yeron' instead of 'ió' and 'ieron.'

- Yo leí
- Ella leyó
- Nosotros leímos
- Ellos leyeron.

Let's look at a few examples.

- Present- Yo como manzanas.
- Past- Yo comí manzanas.

- Present- Ellos escriben en el papel.
- Past- Ellos escribieron en el papel.

Practice reading aloud the following sentences.

Ellos trabajaron de nueve a cuatro.
Mi familia cenó temprano anoche.
Yo gané cien dólares ayer.

They worked from nine to four.
My family had dinner early last night.
I earned one hundred dollars yesterday.

Turn these present-tense sentences into past tense.

- Yo dejo mis llaves en la mesa.

_____

- Ellos no comen nada.

_____

- Nosotros llamamos a nuestra madre.

_____

- Tú esperas mucho tiempo.

_____

- Yo camino mucho.

_____

- El trabaja poco.

_____

- Los niños saltan en el parque.

_____

- Mis vecinos miran una película en el cine.

_____

- Rita y Josefina pasean en el centro comercial.

_____

- La cocinera prepara unos pasteles exquisitos.

_____

Practice

Answering Questions in Past Tense

Now that you can put on past tense endings instead of the present, let's practice answering some questions using the past tense.

¿A qué hora cenaste anoche? (What time did you have dinner last night?)

_____

¿Cuándo estudiaste español? (When did you study Spanish?)

_____

¿A quién llamaste ayer? (Who did you call yesterday?)

_____

¿Qué comiste de almuerzo? (What did you eat for lunch?)

_____

¿Cuándo llegaron tus amigos? (When did your friends arrive?)

_____

Let's practice. For this next exercise, you must first recognize and change the verb tense, moving these sentences into present or past tense.

Ellos estudiaron mucho. _____

Manejé por cinco horas. _____

Yo no escribí mucho. _____

Nosotros trabajamos en el campo. _____

Tú recibiste cien dólares por tu trabajo. _____

Él llevó fruta al picnic. _____

Ella tomó el bus en frente de la tienda. _____

The irregular verbs

Not every verb follows the same rules. We have many irregular verbs in English, but there are only a few common and irregular verbs in Spanish. As we begin with ser and estar, let's see the past tense of both verbs.

Verbo ser

Yo era	fui	Nosotros éramos	fuimos
Tú eras	fuiste	Ustedes eran	fueron
Ella/el/usted era	fue	Ellos/ellas eran	fueron

Verbo estar

Yo	estuve	Nosotros	estuvimos
Tú	estuviste	Ustedes	estuvieron
Ella/él/usted	estuvo	Ellos/ellas	estuvieron

Let's go over another two important ones. *Ir* means 'to go', and hacer means 'to do.' As you already know, these two verbs are also irregular in the present tense. In the past tense, *ir* becomes-

Verbo ir (to go)

Yo	fui	Nosotros	fuimos
Tú	fuiste	Ustedes	fueron
Ella/él/usted	fue	Ellos/ellas	fueron

Even though the root becomes completely different, the endings follow the same pattern (mostly) as what you have learned already. As you may have noticed, the neat thing about this verb in the past is that it stands for two things. It can be *ir-* to go, but it can also be *ser-* to be.

How do we know which is which? We just have to look at the words around it. Look at this sentence.

- Yo fui al gimnasio.

Would it make more sense to say I went to the gym or I was to the gym?

The first one is the only one that makes sense. It will be the same with other sentences, meaning one less verb form for you to memorize.

Read the following sentences and determine if the verb stands for went or was/ were.

a. Ellos fueron maestros antes.
b. Yo fui al parque.
c. Tú fuiste muy amable.
d. Nosotros fuimos a la tienda en la noche.
e. Usted fue a la clase.

Verbo hacer (to do)

Yo	hice	Nosotros	hicimos
Tú	hiciste	Ustedes	hicieron
Ella/él/usted	hizo	Ellos/ellas	hicieron

Once again, even though the root changes, the endings mostly follow the same pattern.

Read aloud these questions.

- ¿Qué hiciste anoche?- What did you do last night?
- ¿Quién hizo el pastel?- Who made the cake? (Note that when we don't know who did an action, we use the él/ ella conjugation)
- ¿Dónde hiciste tu trabajo?- Where did you do your work?

There are several more irregular verbs, but we won't review each individually. Instead, I will list the verb and its root here. You can conjugate the rest of it on your own.

- Querer- to want (quis-)
- Poner- to put (pus-)
- Tener- to have (tuv-)
- Saber- to know (sup-)
- Decir- to say (dij-)
- Estar- to be (estuv-)
- Poder- to be able to (pud-)
- Traer- to bring (traj-)

Time phrases that can be used with the Past Tenses

Yesterday	Ayer
The day before yesterday	Anteayer
Last night	Anoche o ayer a la noche
Last week	La semana pasada
Last weekend	El fin de semana pasado
Last month	El mes pasado
Last year	El año pasado
Last summer	El verano pasado
A year, a month, a day ago	Hace un año, un mes, un día
Two, three, four days, weeks, years ago	Hace dos, tres, cuastro días, semanas, años
Yesterday morning	Ayer a la mañana

LET'S PRACTICE!

Irregular past-tense practice

Practice reading and understanding a few sentences using regular irregular past tense verbs.

- Ellos trajeron comida a la fiesta. _____
- Nosotros quisimos trabajar menos. _____
- Yo dije que no. _____
- Ellos estuvieron muy cansados durante todo el día. _____
_____
- Tú no pudiste abrir el libro. _____
- Ella tuvo una fiesta. _____
- Nosotros no pudimos estudiar. _____
- Tú dijiste que no. _____
- Ellos pusieron la ropa en la cama. _____
- Yo traje mi libro a la clase. _____

CHAPTER 14

REVIEWING PREVIOUS CHAPTERS

Actively studying is much better for our brains than passively studying. With passive studying, we stare at a page of words with their translations and read them. Our brains aren't having to work at anything, so that isn't as effective. With active studying, we are making our brains work for the answers.

LET'S PRACTICE!

So, to start connecting all we have been learning, let´s begin with a brief warm-up.

Me llamo …………………………………………… y tengo …………………………………
años. Mi cumpleaños es el ……………………………………………………Vivo……
en …………………………………….. Me gusta………………………………………………
…………………………………………………………… pero no me gusta
……………………….. …………………………………………………….. Mi actividad
favorita es ……………………………………………………………………………………
…………………………………….. y mis colores preferidos son …………………………
……………………………………………………

What time is it?

Complete the table writing the time with numbers or letters.

Son las doce.	
	2:50
Son las cinco y media.	
	8:10
Es la una.	
	3:25
Son las diez y cuarto.	
	4:30
Son las ocho y cuarenta.	
	11:40

What day is today?

Complete the table writing the time with numbers or letters.

Hoy es lunes 3 de noviembre	3/11
	5/10
La fecha es martes 25 de septiembre	
	16/8
Hoy es sábado 7 de diciembre	
	1/1
La fecha es jueves 15 de febrero	
	4/5
Hoy es domingo 19 de agosto	
	7/6

There are so many ways we can review our knowledge. We can make flashcards (preferably looking at the English side so that we have to work to recall the Spanish side) or listen to someone asking questions and try to reply with the answers. Anything that makes our brains think is better than just reading the words off the page.

Pronouns, nouns, and adjectives

Connect with lines

Esas	niño	juguetón
Estas	manzanas	favorita
Mi	señor	gigante
El	plantas	deliciosas
Ese	pelota	enfermo
Aquella	perro	perfumadas
Una	casa	educado
Un	ballena	coqueta
Nuestra	señora	entrenado
Esa	atleta	blanca

Singular, plural, masculine or feminine

Mark with an X in the correct columns

Palabra	singular	plural	femenino	masculino
toalla	X		X	
chocolates				
manzanas				
silla				
perros				
cocodrilo				
frutas				
máquina				
teléfonos				
botellas				

Subjects, verbs, and pronouns

Identify the verb and the subject of each pair of sentences and
write the correct pronoun in the second one.

- Javier es mi mejor amigo. ....es de Madrid, España.
- María y Julieta juegan tenis. ....no son jugadoras profesionales.
- Francisco tiene un regalo muy especial. ....está muy feliz.
- Alicia y Laura son de Costa Rica. ....bailan salsa todos los días.
- Ricardo es profesor de Química. ....trabaja siempre en el laboratorio.
- Juan y Patricio son compañeros de clase. .... son de México.

Choose the best answer for each question

¿Cuántos años tienes? •	• Es el 16 de septiembre.
¿Cómo es ese niño? •	• Yo quiero comer pizza y helado.
¿Quién es tu mejor amigo? •	• Tengo cuarenta y dos años.
¿Te gustó la película? •	• Sí. Le encantó. Dijo que estaba delicioso.
¿Cuándo es la Independencia de México? •	• Es muy tranquilo y alegre.
¿Le gustó el pastel a Rodrigo? •	• Llega a las 3:40 PM.
¿Quién quiere comer pizza? •	• Se llama Nicolás González. Es de Perú.
¿Cuándo viene el tren? •	• No me gustó. Era muy aburrida.

Answer Some Questions

Practice answering these questions.
Look back at the previous chapters if you have any questions.

- ¿Cómo te llamas?

  _____

- ¿Cuántos años tienes?

  _____

- ¿Tienes mascotas?

  _____

- ¿Necesitas estudiar?

  _____

- ¿Te gusta el español?

  _____

- ¿Qué hora es?

  _____

- ¿Cuándo es tu cumpleaños?

  _____

- ¿Dónde está tu casa?

  _____

- ¿Por qué estudias español?

  _____

- ¿Adónde fuiste ayer?

  _____

- ¿Qué hiciste el domingo?

  _____

- ¿Cómo eres tú?

  _____

- ¿Cómo se llama tu mejor amigo? ¿Qué le gusta hacer?

  _____

Using the verbs in the correct tense

Complete the paragraph

Yo (ser) .... Mario y (jugar) .... al fútbol todos los domingos. Me gusta jugar cuando (hacer) .... frío y poco calor. Mi mejor amigo se (llamar) .... Pedro. Él (practicar) .... natación. Así que cuando yo (terminar) .... de jugar fútbol, (ir) .... a la piscina y los dos juntos (nadar) .... un rato. Los sábados (ir) .... al centro comercial y (almorzar) .... ahí hamburguesas. Cuando nosotros (regresar) ...., (invitar) .... a nuestros amigos a mi casa. Pedro (tocar) .... la guitarra y yo (cantar) .... Nuestros amigos (bailar) .... y todos nos (reir) .... mucho. Por las noches todos juntos (ir) .... a fiestas y nos (divertir) .... mucho. Los domingos (descansar) .... Me gusta (tener) .... amigos como ellos.

Talking About Your Town

In this section, we will focus on what you learned in chapter eleven, so if you need to review that vocabulary, feel free to flip back and look.

Answer these questions about your city.

- ¿Hay museos en tu ciudad?

_____

- ¿Hay una clase de español?

_____

- ¿Qué te gusta visitar en tu ciudad?

_____

- ¿Qué está en frente de tu casa?

_____

- ¿Hay muchas personas en tu ciudad?

_____

Answer these questions about yourself.

• ¿Qué te gusta desayunar?

_____

• ¿A qué hora te gusta estudiar?

_____

• ¿Qué tipo de música te gusta escuchar?

_____

• ¿Te molesta el frío?

_____

• ¿Con quién te gusta viajar?

_____

Complete the missing word.

1. A nosotros _____ gusta tu apartamento.
2. Me _____ ir de vacaciones contigo.
3. A mi mamá _____ encanta la comida italiana.
4. ¿Te _____ los libros de cocina?
5. A mí _____ fastidia tanto tráfico.

Answers: **1.** nos; **2.** gusta/encanta; **3.** le; **4.** interesan/gustan; **5.** me

Past Tense Review

In this exercise, you will practice what you learned in chapter thirteen. As you read the sentences and comprehend the meaning of each one, find the verb in the past.

6. Tú _____ (vender) tu casa vieja.
7. Mis hermanos y yo _____ (ir) a la escuela el viernes.
8. Mi padre _____ (comer) toda la comida.
9. Yo _____ (estudiar) después de la escuela.
10. Lucía _____ (beber) jugo.
11. Juan y Julio _____ (ir) a ver una película.
12. Hoy, yo _____ (hacer) mi tarea temprano.
13. Los estudiantes _____ (poner) su tarea en el escritorio.
14. Eduardo _____ (tener) una mascota antes.
15. Tú _____ (olvidar) estudiar para el examen.

FAMILY

A little bit of Latino culture

In English-speaking cultures, we are often very particular about how we relate to someone. "Well, she's my cousin's child, so she's not my cousin, she's my cousin once removed," you might say to explain the relationship.

However, by watching movies, meeting Latino people or reading books, it is easy to understand that family is a core and key support and guidance in Latin American society. Latinos families are very close and tend to live in the same city, area, or region. The main point of this type of family is spending time together, and supporting each other. In Spanish-speaking cultures, nobody worries about the exact relationship between families. A cousin is a cousin. Maybe it's someone's second cousin, or their niece or nephew, but because they are similar in age, they may call them cousin instead.

Most Latinos have two last names, one from their father and one from their mother. When Latino women marry, they generally don't change their names. Sometimes, they might add on "de Gutiérrez" or "de Moreno" at the end of their name, but there is usually no legal changing of names.

If someone has two last names, you might ask yourself, how do they know which one to pass on? They always pass on their "first" last name, which comes from their father's side of the family.

For example, if a person named Silvia Jiron Duarte was married to someone named Silvio Obando Gutiérrez, then their child would be _____ Obando Jiron.

If you were born in a Latino culture, your name would be _____ (first name) _____ (last name) _____ (mother's maiden name). When or if you have children, you would pass on that first last name and so would your spouse.

Because Latinos typically have two last names, they don't always have a middle name. It's not strange for them to have a middle name, but it's also not something every child has, like in most English-speaking countries.

Family Vocabulary

Before we get into our list of new words, remember that many of these will be similar because sometimes in Spanish all you have to do to change a word from masculine to feminine is change the last letter. That should make memorization easier. Instead of "uncle" and "aunt," two vastly different words, we have tio and tia. Good luck!

Papá	Father	Primo	Cousin	Hijo	Son
Mamá	Mother	Prima	Cousin	Hija	Daughter
Hermano	Brother	Bisabuela	Great grandmother	Sobrino	Nephew
Hermana	Sister	Bisabuelo	Great grandfather	Sobrina	Niece
Abuelo	Grandfather	Padrastro	Stepfather	Cuñado	Brother in law
Abuela	Grandmother	Madrastra	Stepmother	Cuñada	Sister in law
Tío	Uncle	Hermanastro	Stepbrother	Suegro	Father in law
Tía	Aunt	Hermanastra	Stepsister	Suegra	Mother in law
Esposo	Husband	Esposa	Wife	Novio	Boyfriend
Novia	Girlfriend	Comprometido	Engaged	Nuera	Daughter in law
Nieto	Grandson	Nieta	Granddaughter	Yerno	Son in law

Let´s discover together this family tree.

	Nora, esposa de Eduardo, mamá de Estela y Fernanda, suegra de Rodolfo y Diego y abuela de Paola, Carlos, María, Susana, Gonzalo, Carlos, Inés, Andrea, Pedro y Alberto.	Eduardo, esposo de Nora, papá de Estela y Fernanda, suegro de Rodolfo y Diego y abuelo de Paola, Carlos, María, Susana, Gonzalo, Carlos, Inés, Andrea, Pedro y Alberto.	
Mi papá Rodolfo, esposo de Estela, yerno de Nora y Eduardo, tío de Gonzalo, Carlos, Inés, Andrea, Pedro y Alberto, cuñado de Fernanda y Diego y papá de Paola, Carlos, María y Susana.		Mi tía Fernanda, hermana de mi mamá, hija de mis abuelos Nora y Eduardo, esposa de Diego y cuñada de Rodolfo, mamá de Gonzalo, Carlos, Inés, Andrea, Pedro y Alberto y tía de Paola, Carlos, María y Susana.	Mi tío Diego, esposo de mi tía Fernanda, yerno de Nora y Eduardo, cuñado de Estela y Rodolfo, papá de Gonzalo, Carlos, Inés, Andrea, Pedro y Alberto y tío de Paola, Carlos, María y Susana.

Yo Paola	Mi hermano mayor Carlos	Mi hermana menor María	Mi hermana Susana	Mi primo Gonzalo	Mi primo Carlos	Mi prima Inés	Mi prima Andrea	Mi primo Pedro	Mi primo Alberto

Nietos de Nora y Eduardo Hijos de Estela y Rodolfo Primos de Gonzalo, Carlos, Inés, Andrea, Pedro y Alberto.	Nietos de Nora y Eduardo Hijos de Fernanda y Diego Primos de Paola, Carlos, María y Susana.

LET'S PRACTICE!

Family Vocabulary Practice

Based on the tree, who is who?

1. ¿Quién es la hermana de Fernanda?

....

2. ¿Quiénes son las hermanas de Carlos?

....

3. ¿Quién es el esposo de Nora?

....

4. ¿Quién es el papá de Alberto?

....

5. ¿Quién es la tía de Carlos?

....

6. ¿Quién es el abuelo de Pedro?

....

7. ¿Quién es el cuñado de Diego?

....

8. ¿Quién es la cuñada de Rodolfo?

....

9. ¿Quiénes son los primos de Inés?

....

10. ¿Quiénes son las primas de Paola?

....

LET'S PRACTICE!

Actividades en familia

Complete using the correct conjugation of the present tense and read aloud.

Las familias latinas (ser) ………………… muy unidas y les (gustar) …………………
(hacer) ………………… muchas actividades juntos. (Pasear) …………………
todos juntos, (celebrar) ………………… cumpleaños y se (visitar) …………………
con frecuencia. (ser) ………………… familias que se (acompañar) …………………
y se (ayudar) ………………… y a menudo (vivir) ………………… cerca.

Solve the following riddles and guess which family member is being described.

1. Es el hermano de tu mamá. _____
2. Es el papá de tu papá. _____
3. Es la hija de tu mamá. _____
4. Es el hijo de tu hermano. _____
5. Es el hermano de tu esposo. _____

Complete this dialogue between two brothers using the verbs in the box.

> CREO - FUE – TUVE – ESTUVO – JUGUEMOS - TENGO - NECESITO – PREPARÓ
> – ESTÁ – QUIERES – VISITAR-   ESTUDIAR- ESTÁ – REGRESA - FUE

Juan: ¡Hola José! ¿Cómo te …………………en la escuela?
José: …………………que bien. …………………un examen de Química y
………………… estudiar para mi prueba de Biología que será mañana. ¿Y tú?
Juan: Mi día ………………… muy bueno pero ………………… mucha hambre.
José: Mamá ………………… un pastel de coco. …………………delicioso.
Juan: ¡Que rico! ¡Gracias! ¿………………… jugar un rato afuera en el parque?
José: ………………… un rato porque tengo que …………………
Juan: ¿Sabes dónde ………………… mamá?
José: Sí, ella se ………………… a ………………… a la tía Elena.

Answer these questions about your family.

1. ¿Cuántos hermanos tienes? _____
2. ¿Tu familia es grande o pequeña? _____
3. ¿Cómo es tu tío? _____
4. ¿Tienes sobrinos? _____

Family Vocabulary Reading

Read this little story about a family. There may be a few
words you don't recognize in this story. Try to use the
words around them to give you a hint about what they might mean.

*Hola, me llamo Marta. Tengo veinte años y estudio en la universidad. Hoy
quiero hablar sobre mi familia. Mi mamá es Verónica y mi papá se llama Carlos.
Yo tengo dos hermanos mayores, Martín y Francisco. Tienen veinticuatro y
veintidós años. No tengo hermanas.*

*Nosotros vivimos en una casa cerca de la casa de mis primos. Me gusta mucho
visitar, pasear y jugar con mis primos. Tengo cuatro primos. Nicolás tiene
dieciocho años, María tiene quince; Pedro tiene doce y Valeria tiene ocho.
Valeria es baja y tiene pelo castaño, A Valeria le gusta jugar a las escondidas.
Normalmente, ella se esconde y yo la busco en la casa.*

—¿Qué haces? —pregunta mi tío.
—No sé dónde está Valeria.
—Ella está en…
—¡Shhh! —escucho desde el baño.

Yo sé dónde está mi prima. Ella está encima del lavamanos.

1. ¿Cuántos años tienen los hermanos de Marta?

_____

2. ¿Cuántos primos tiene?

_____

3. ¿A qué le gusta jugar a Valeria?

_____

4. ¿Dónde busca Marta?

_____

5. ¿Quién ayuda a Marta?

_____

CHAPTER 16

PLACES AND PARTS OF THE HOMES WHERE FAMILIES LIVE

There are many places to put down roots around the world. People have been living in homes no matter the culture or the country and adapting their needs to the weather their places have. Houses come in all sizes and shapes. You can live in:

Las montañas	The mountains	Condominio	Condominium
Las ciudades	The cities	Casa de campo	Country house
El campo	The camp	Choza	Hut
La granja	The farm	Albergue	Shelter
Un apartamento	An apartment	Carpa	Tent
Una casa	A house	Rancho	Ranch
Un barco	A boat	Casa marítima	Sea house
Una cabaña	A cottage	Casa rodante	Motorhome

LET'S PRACTICE!

¿Dónde vives?
Yo vivo en un apartamento pequeño con vista al mar.

¿Cuál es tu lugar favorito para vivir?
....

¿Te gustan las casas rodantes o las casas de campo?
....

¿Prefieres vivir en una casa o un apartamento?
....

Parts of a home

A typical house has the following spaces:

Las escaleras	The stairs	El dormitorio	The bedroom
El ascensor	The elevator	El pasillo	The hallway
El comedor	The dining room	La terraza	The terrace
El baño	The bathroom	El jardín	The garden
La cocina	The kitchen	El ático	The attic
El garaje	The garage	El sótano	The basement
La sala	The living room	El techo	The roof
La oficina	The office	La lavandería	The laundry room

Kitchen items

El horno	The oven	La cuchara	The spoon
La nevera	The fridge	El cuchillo	The knife
La cafetera	The coffee maker	El tenedor	The fork
La batidora	The blender	El vaso	The glass
El lavaplatos	The dishwasher	El plato	The plate
El Lavabo	The sink	La taza	The cup
El microondas	The microwave	La olla	The pot
El mesón	The counter	La sartén	The pan
La mesa	The table	La silla	The chair
La tostadora	The toaster	El grifo	The faucet
El mantel	The tablecloth	El basurero	The trash can
El paño de cocina	The kitchen towel	La servilleta	The napkin
La tabla de cortar	The cutting board	El tazón	The bowl
Las alacenas	The cupboards	Los frascos	The jars
El detergente	The detergent	La esponja	The sponge

Living room items

La mesita	The coffee table	El televisor	The TV
La ventana	The window	La lámpara	The lamp
Las cortinas	The curtains	La chimenea	The chimney
El teléfono	The phone	El cuadro	The painting
La alfombra	The carpet	La biblioteca	The bookcase
El cojín	The cushion	El reloj	The clock
El sillón	The couch	Los libros	The books
Las fotografías	The photographs	Las plantas	The plants
El control remoto	The remote control	La puerta	The door
El florero	The flowerpot	Las llaves	The keys

Bathroom items

El inodoro	The toilet	El espejo	The mirror
La ducha	The shower	El jabón	The soap
El Grifo	The tap	El cepillo de dientes	The toothbrush
La bañera	The tub	El papel higiénico	The toilet paper
El secador	The hair dryer	La pasta de dientes	The toothpaste
La toalla	The towel	El peine	The comb

Bedroom items

La cama	The bed	Los juguetes	The toys
La mesa de noche	The night table	El colchón	The mattress
El armario	The closet	La almohada	The pillow
El escritorio	The desk	El oso de peluche	The teddy bear
La percha	The hanger	La muñeca	The doll
La cuna	The crib	El reloj despertador	The alarm clock
Las sábanas	The sheets	La luz de mesa	The table light
El edredón	The comforter	El ventilador	The fan

Random items we have in our houses

La aspiradora	The vacuum cleaner	Las luces	The lights
Las cajas	The boxes	El timbre	The bell
El enchufe	The plug	La escoba	The broom
Los juegos de mesa	The table games	Las herramientas	The tools

Adjectives to describe our homes

Luminosa/o	Luminous	Fría/o	Cold
Grande	Big	Linda/o	Nice
Pequeña/o	Small, little	Fea/o	Ugly
Moderna/o	Modern	Vieja/o	Old
Desordenado/a	Untidy	Cómoda/o	Comfortable
Cálida/o	Warm	Ordenada	Tidy

Activities at home

Cortar el césped	To mow the lawn	Hacer mercado	To do the groceries
Pasar la aspiradora	To vacuum	Sacar la basura	To take out the trash
Limpiar el baño	To clean the bathroom	Ordenar	To order
Lavar los platos	To wash the dishes	Barrer	To sweep
Cocinar	To cook	Hacer las camas	To make the beds
Limpiar la cocina	To clean the kitchen	Arreglar la sala	To tidy up the room

It is a lot of new vocabulary so let´s practice!
Where is it? Complete the sentences with the right place.

- Los platos están en ………………………………….
- La ducha está en ………………………………..
- Las sábanas están en ………………………………….
- El microondas está en …………………………………..
- El sillón está en …………………………………..
- La cama está en …………………………………..
- Los juguetes están en …………………………………..
- Los carros están en …………………………………..
- Los cuchillos están en …………………………………..
- La toalla está en …………………………………..
- Los osos de peluche están en …………………………………..

Tres objetos que encontramos en

La cocina	La sala	El dormitorio

Tres objetos que NO encontramos en

El baño	El parque	El garaje

Tres objetos de la casa que empiezan con la letra

A	M	S

Tres objetos de la casa que terminan con la letra

R	O	N

Is it V (VERDADERO) (TRUE) or F (FALSO) (FALSE). Mark the correct V or F

F	
	Hay una cama y un papel higiénico en el jardín de mi casa.
	Hay una almohada y un colchón en el dormitorio de mi casa.
	Hay un sillón en la cocina de mi casa.
	Hay un microondas en el baño de mi casa.
	Hay un refrigerador en mi dormitorio.
	Hay una mesa y una silla en la cocina de mi casa.
	Hay una cafetera y un cuchillo en el jardín de mi casa.

Adjectives that describe your home. Circle those that apply. Mi casa es

luminosa	grande	linda	fría
pequeña	moderna	vieja	fea
desordenada	cálida	ordenada	cómoda

Mi casa es ....
....

Adjectives that describe your bedroom. Circle those that apply. Mi dormitorio es

luminoso	grande	lindo	frío
pequeño	moderno	Viejo	feo
desordenado	cálido	Ordenado	cómodo

Mi dormitorio es ....
....

Home activities. Who does what? Complete the chart with the person who does this task at your house.

Cortar el césped		Hacer las compras	
Pasar la aspiradora		Sacar la basura	
Limpiar el baño		Ordenar	
Lavar los platos		Barrer	
Cocinar		Hacer las camas	
Limpiar la cocina		Arreglar la sala	

Now write the sentences indicating who in your family does each task. For example. Mi papa corta el césped.

....
....
....
....
....
....
....
....
....
....
....

Prepositions

Prepositions or las preposiciones are short words usually used with nouns and pronouns to give information about direction, location, time, manner, reason or introduce an object. They can be simple prepositions or prepositional phrases (frases preposicionales) like these examples:

Preposiciones	Frases preposicionales
- en la cama	- debajo de la mesa
- a las 12:45hs	- encima de la silla
- por la puerta	- dentro de la heladera

Preposition List

Preposición	English	Use	Example
A	At	For times	A las 14:45hs
	To	From…to…	marzo a julio
Ante	Before/in front	In front of/in the presence of	Ante la autoridad/ Ante su padre
Bajo	Down	Toward/ in a lower position	Bajo la lluvia/ Bajo la mesa
Con	With	With someone/in a certain way/	Con su papá/ con alegría
Contra	Against	Against something	Contra su idea
De	From	From… to…	De 7 a 8/ de lunes a sábado
Desde	Since	Starting at a certain point or time	Desde mi casa/ desde la tarde
Durante	During	Length of time	Durante la pandemia
En	In	Places/times	En Barcelona/en 1967/ en verano/en enero
Entre	Between	Between two things	Entre enero y marzo/ entre la mesa y la silla/ entre la pelota y la bicicleta
Hacia	Towards	In the direction of	Hacia el Sur
Hasta	By/until	By or until a certain point or time	Hasta la pared/ hasta febrero
Mediante	Through	Across, over	Mediante muchas reuniones
Para	For, in order to	Recipient	Una camisa para mi hermano

Por	By, reason for something	Reason for something, means of something	Dos veces por día/ indicado por un doctor
Según	According to	Depending on/ in conformity with	Según las investigaciones
Sin	Without	Missing an object, a reason, a person	Sin casco/sin excusas/ sin su perro
Sobre	About, on	Referring to someone or something	Un libro sobre Egipto
Tras	Behind	Behind something or someone	Tras la montaña
Versus	Versus	Opposition/ confrontation	Warriors versus Chicago Bulls
Via	By	Going through/ stopover	Vía Madrid

LET'S PRACTICE!

Find the preposition in each sentence.

- Yo voy a la biblioteca para leer en silencio.
- Yo camino alrededor de la cancha de béisbol cuando no llueve.
- Yo estoy con mis amigos desde las diez de la mañana.
- Yo juego contra ellos bajo presión.
- Yo soy de los Estados Unidos.
- El título del libro es interesante, pero entre nosotros, es muy aburrido.
- Llueve desde ayer a la noche.
- El lápiz está bajo la silla.
- El cuaderno azúl está en la mochila de mi amigo.
- Ellos están en clase de Biología.
- Yo no puedo escoger entre la manzana y la naranja.
- El gato está sobre el sofá.
- Mis vecinos están sin mi ayuda para preparar el festival.
- El juguete está entre la caja y la silla.
- Yo trabajo hasta las cinco de la tarde.
- La comida es para mí porque estoy sin almorzar.
- Me gusta el café sin azúcar.
- El cielo gris está sobre las montañas.
- El avión vuela hacia Miami con escala en Panamá.
- Elizabeth está en contra de tu opinión.
- Según los médicos, su estado de salud es estable, pero sigue delicado.
- La masa se trabaja mediante golpes suaves.
- Lo de siempre: Oriente versus Occidente.
- Hubo muchos gritos y golpes durante el partido de fútbol.

Let's practice using these prepositions.

Read the sentences below and figure out which preposition would be appropriate to complete the sentence. In some cases, more than one might fit depending on what you want to say.

- Yo camino de mi casa _____ mi trabajo. (hint- if you're going from one place, it would only make sense that you are going to another place)
- Ellos toman su café _____ azúcar. (hint- they don't like sugar)
- El perro está _____ su casa. (hint- the dog doesn't like the cold outside)
- El techo (ceiling or roof) está _____ las camas. (hint- where would it make sense for the roof to be in relation to the beds?)
- La farmacia está _____ las dos tiendas. (hint- there is a store on either side of the pharmacy)

Read the following sentences out loud

- Por suerte, terminé mi tarea temprano.
- Los estudiantes están dentro de la clase.
- Por ejemplo, yo soy más alto.
- Ellos traen la tarea para la clase.
- Nosotros somos de México.
- El lápiz está sobre el escritorio.

Contractions

A contraction is where two words are joined to form a single one. In Spanish there are only two recognized forms of contractions:

- AL (A+EL) (formed by the preposition A plus the article EL.
- DEL (DE+EL) (formed by the preposition DE plus the article EL)

Reading Comprehension

Read the following paragraph and answer the questions about what it says. Most of the words are ones you have learned, but a few new ones are scattered throughout. Feel free to look them up if you don't remember them!

Hola, me llamo Marcos y soy de Florida. Tengo quince años y voy al colegio San Juan. Yo estudio inglés, pero no soy muy bueno. Mi familia va a mudarse a una casa nueva y estoy emocionado. Yo fui a la casa nueva anoche y me gustó mucho.

La casa nueva tiene cuatro dormitorios y tres baños. Tiene un sótano también. La casa nueva es más grande que la casa que tengo ahora. Mamá quiso comprar muchas cosas para la nueva casa. Quiso comprar dos camas nuevas, más un sofá. Yo quiero una televisión para mi dormitorio, pero me dijo que no.

Vamos a mudarnos el quince de febrero.

¿Cuántos dormitorios hay en la casa nueva? _____

¿Hay un sótano o un ático en la casa? _____

¿Qué quiso comprar la madre? _____

¿Cuándo se mudan? _____

House Practice

Read the following sentences and take them as an example.

Mi casa tiene dos baños. Un baño está cerca de la cocina y el otro baño está cerca de mi dormitorio. En mi dormitorio hay dos lámparas y una cama. La cama es grande y rosada. No tengo alfombra en mi dormitorio. Hay otro dormitorio, pero lo uso como oficina. Tengo un escritorio y una silla. También, mi computadora está allí. Hay una televisión en mi sala, pero no hay televisión en mi dormitorio.

Write a description of where you live. Add as many details as you like.

....
....
....
....
....
....
....
....
....
....

CHAPTER 17

LET'S GO SHOPPING

In this chapter, we will prepare for one of the things you can't avoid when going somewhere no matter how well you packed: shopping.

There is no exact translation for the word to shop. In Spanish, you have to use the phrase *ir de compras*. You already know the names of lots of different types of stores. Some of these are:

Farmacia	Gasolinera	Librería	Centro Comercial

However, there are a few more places you might go to as well.

Stores

El mercado	El supermercado	La tienda	El almacén
The market	*The supermarket*	*The store*	*The corner store*

La zapatería	La panadería	La carnicería	La boutique
The shoe store	*The bakery*	*The butcher shop*	*Ladies clothing shop*

La sastrería	La juguetería	Mercado de agricultores	La óptica
The tailor's shop	*The toy store*	*The farmer's market*	*Eye doctor*

La pescadería	La florería	La ferretería	La heladería
The fishmonger's	*The flower shop*	*The hardware store*	*The ice cream parlor*

La licorería	El barbero	La cerrajería	La tintorería
The liquor store	*The barber*	*The locksmith's shop*	*The dry cleaners*

- El mercado is typically an outdoor market with different vendors. Most of the vendors sell food.

- El almacén is typically in neighborhoods and not in a main part of town. It carries necessities like milk, fruits and vegetables, oil, diapers, etc.

Now, get ready for all the new vocabulary you will find here. What can you find in each store? We will begin with the Supermercado since it's the biggest and inside it we can find many interesting sections.

Shopping for groceries

Supermercado			

Secos/dry		Lácteos/diary	
Café	Coffee	Crema	Cream
Azúcar	Sugar	Huevo	Egg
Arroz	Rice	Leche	Milk
Avena	Oatmeal	Mantequilla	Butter
Aceite	Oil	Queso	Cheese
Aderezos	Salad dressing	Queso requesón	Cottage cheese
Cereales	Cereal	Yogur	Yogurt
Copetín	Snacks	Verdulería/Vegetables	
Galletas	Cookies	Alcachofa	Artichoke
Lata de tomate	Can of Tomatoes	Apio	Celery
Mostaza	Mustard	Berenjena	Eggplant
Sal	Salt	Cebolla	Onion
Puré	Purée	Champiñones	Mushrooms
Garbanzos	Chickpeas	Espárragos	Asparagus
Té	Tea	Espinaca	Spinach
Harina	Flour	Frijoles	Beans
Pimienta	Pepper	Lechuga	Lettuce
Lentejas	Lentils	Maíz	Corn
Semillas	Seeds	Patatas	Potatoes
Mayonesa	Mayonnaise	Pepino	Cucumber
Pasta	Pasta	Pimiento	Pepper
Sopas	Soups	Rúcula	Arugula
Vinagre	Vinegar	Tomate	Tomato
Lata de atún	Can of Tuna	Zanahoria	Carrot

Frutas/fruits		Carne/meat	
Arándano	Blueberry	Carne de res	Beef
Kiwi	Kiwi	Cerdo	Pork
Limón	Lemon	Conejo	Rabbit
Fresa	Strawberry	Cordero	Lamb
Pera	Pear	Costillas	Ribs
Naranja	Orange	Hamburguesa	Hamburger
Durazno	Peach	Jamón	Ham
Plátano	Banana	Lomo	Loin
Piña	Pineapple	Muslo	Thigh

Mandarina	Tangerine		Pavo	Turkey
Uvas	Grapes		Pechuga	Breast
Ciruelas	Plum		Pescado	Fish
Cereza	Cherry		Pollo	Chicken
Melón	Melon		Salchicha	Sausage
Sandía	Watermelon		Solomillo	Sirloin
Manzana	Apple		Ternera	Veal

Limpieza/Cleaning			Perfumería/perfumery/toiletries	
Desodorante	Deodorant		Acondicionador	Conditioner
Desinfectante	Disinfectant		Algodón	Cotton
Mopa	Swab		Cepillo	Brush
Escoba	Broom		Cepillo de dientes	Toothbrush
Bolsa de basura	Garbage bag		Champú	Shampoo
Paños	Clothes		Crema corporal	Body cream
Toalla de papel	Paper towel		Hisopo	Cotton swab
Jabón	Soap		Jabón	Soap
Pañuelos	Tissue		Maquillaje	Makeup
Lavandina	Bleach		Pañales	Diapers
Detergente	Detergent		Pasta de dientes	Toothpaste
Esponja	Sponge		Peine	Comb
Pala	Shovel		Perfumes	Perfumes
Servilletas de papel	Napkins		Toallas húmedas	Wet towels

Panadería/Bakery			Congelados /Frozen	
Galletas	Cookies		Comidas congeladas	Frozen foods
Rosquillas	Donuts		Frutas congeladas	Frozen fruits
Sandwiches	Sandwiches		Helados	Ice Cream
Tartas	Tarts		Patatas congeladas	Frozen potatoes
Pan	Bread		Vegetales congelados	Frozen veggies
Medialunas	Croissants		Rotisería/Deli	
Tortas	Cakes		Pollo rostizado	Roasted Chicken
Magdalenas	Cupcakes		Pollo frito	Fried chicken
Pizza	Pizza		Patatas fritas	Fried potatoes
Tostadas	Toast		Ensaladas	Salads

Otros productos/other items

Focos de luz	Light bulb	Gelatina	Jelly
Fósforos	Matches	Miel	Honey
Gaseosa	Sodas	Vino blanco	White wine
Papel aluminio	Foil paper	Postres	Desserts
Velas	Candles	Mezcla para paste	Cake mix
Vino tinto	Red wine	Jugo	Juice

LET´S PRACTICE!

Connect with lines. Where do you buy…

Pan y medialunas? •	• La juguetería
Atún? •	• La panadería
Espinaca, tomate y lechuga? •	• La florería
Bistec de carne? •	• La heladería
Flores? •	• La pescadería
Servilletas de papel? •	• La verdulería
Pelotas de fútbol y robots? •	• La carnicería
Helado de chocolate? •	• El supermercado

Now, it is time to create una "lista de supermercado".

Imagine that you want to bake a birthday cake. You will need eggs, butter, sugar, flour, vanilla, chocolate, cream, and candles. Can you make a list with quantities in Spanish?

- ✓ ....
- ✓ ....
- ✓ ....
- ✓ ....
- ✓ ....
- ✓ ....
- ✓ ....
- ✓ ....

Now, imagine that you want to invite your friends to a pizza night at your house. Make your Spanish list including drinks, appetizers, napkins, and desserts.

....
....
....
....
....
....
....
....
....
....
....
....
....
....

¡SERÁ UNA GRAN NOCHE DE ALEGRÍAS!
(It will be a great night of joy!)

What do you do at a grocery store?

Hacer la compra *To do the shopping*	*Comprar* *To buy*
Pesar las verduras y las frutas *To weigh the vegetables and the fruits*	Pagar *To pay*
Pedir algo en la panadería *To order something at the Bakery*	*Empujar el carrito* *To push the cart*
Tomar un producto *To grab a product*	Comprobar la fecha de caducidad *To check the expiry date*
Esperar en la fila *To wait in the line*	Meter los productos en el carrito *To put the products in the cart*
Pagar con efectivo *To pay with cash*	Pagar con tarjeta *To pay with card*
Pedir el recibo *To ask for the receipt*	Meter los productos en las bolsas *To put the products in the bags*

Here are some sentences that you can read out loud.

Hoy es un día soleado. Son las 8 de la mañana y hace calor. Felipe llega con su carro al supermercado. Busca un carrito y comienza a caminar. Mira su lista de compras en su teléfono y planifica el recorrido por los pasillos. Va primero a la verdulería. Busca las manzanas, unas zanahorias, unos plátanos y la lechuga. Pesa todo en la balanza y mete los productos en el carrito. Su esposa necesita queso. Comprueba la fecha de caducidad y mete el queso junto a las manzanas. También mete huevos, cereales, servilletas de papel y carne. Espera en la fila del cajero. Saca los productos del carrito y paga con tarjeta de crédito. Mete los productos en las bolsas y pide su recibo. Vuelve a su carro y finalmente regresa a su casa.

Now, write your own story.

....
....
....
....
....
....
....
....
....
....
....
....
....
....
....
....

More vocabulary that you will need when shopping.

Caro	Barato	Descuento	Cajero	Cliente	Código de barras
Expensive	Cheap	Discount	Cashier	Client	Bar code

Pasillo	Estante	Canasto	Tarjeta	Precio	Etiqueta
Aisle	Shelf	Basket	Card	Price	Label

Dinero	Monedas	Efectivo	Débito	Probador	Oferta
Money	Coins	Cash	Debit	Fitting room	Offer

Crédito	Recibo	Bolsa	Carrito	Marca	Tallas
Credit	Receipt	Bag	Cart	Brand	Sizes

LET'S PRACTICE!

Find the Spanish words for:

Client	Discount	Cashier	Cash	Label
Brand	Sizes	Offer	Coins	Credit
Fitting room	Cheap	Expensive	Shelf	Basket

```
C V M T E S T A N T E P T I
H A Q B A R A T O C U R F J
O D R C W L J J Q L U O I Q
G T N O R I L M I I H B R D
Q C X T E E L E N E G A T E
E A M E P F D W S N U D Q S
O N M X A O E I T T D O K C
F A R S S Y A C T E X R M U
E S E C I P X G T O N K O E
R T C A L O J V S I K U N N
T O I J L P A L J U V J E T
A E B E O O D A C G H O D O
J B O R E T Q I U E T A A A
I Q H O N I M A R C A M S F
```

Now, let's take a chance to practice this new vocabulary. Read the following sentences.

El sillón es barato.
Compro zapatos negros en la zapatería del Centro Comercial.
Ellos fueron a la gasolinera.
María paga en efectivo.
La fruta está muy cara en el supermercado.
Hay un cliente en el probador.
¿Tiene un talla 14 para mi?

LET'S PRACTICE!

Connect to create sentences.

Compro manzanas •	• para preparar el desayuno de los niños.
Necesitas comprar huevos y leche •	• son deliciosos para preparar un pastel.
María y José •	• en el supermercado.
María usa su tarjeta de crédito •	• caminan por el Centro Comercial.
Esos limones •	• o prefieren pasta para la cena?
¿Les gusta el atún •	• para pagar las compras en la panadería.

Write the complete sentences below:

1.
2.
3.
4.
5.
6.

Now make sentences with these words.

• Tarjeta de débito
_____

• Recibo
_____

• Mercado
_____

• Cajero
_____

• Fuimos
_____

Knowing how to ask about store hours or directions during a Spanish shopping experience is very important. Let´s see:

Entrada	Salida	Horario de atención	Abierto	Cerrado	Feriado
Entrance	Exit	Business hours	Open	Closed	Holiday

So, in Spanish we ask and answer in this way.

- ¿Buen día! ¿Cómo puedo llegar al Centro Comercial?
- Camina derecho dos cuadras y dobla a la izquierda. A media cuadra está la entrada.
- ¡Muchas gracias! ¿Sabes si está abierto ahora?
- ¡Sí! El Centro Comercial abre a las 9 de lunes a viernes. El horario de atención de los días sábados es de 10 a 22hs y los domingos y feriados, el centro está cerrado.
- ¡Genial!¡Gracias por tu ayuda y por toda la información!
- ¡De nada! ¡Que tengas un buen día!
- ¡Y tú también!

LET´S PRACTICE!

Can you answer these questions?

¿Dónde está la entrada del Centro Comercial?

....

¿Cuál es el horario de atención durante los sábados?

....

¿Se puede ir los domingos?

....

Shopping for clothes

There are many fashion words to learn! It is important to learn this vocabulary if you get into a Spanish website or a Spanish-speaking country to buy clothes:

Camiseta	T-shirt	Chaqueta	Jacket	Bufanda	Scarf
Blusa	Blouse	Sostén	Bra	Impermeable	Raincoat
Camisa	Shirt	Vaqueros	Jeans	Poncho	Poncho
Falda	Skirt	Calzoncillos	Underwear	Chanclas	Flip flops
Mini falda	Miniskirt	Bata	Robe	Pantuflas	Slippers
Pantalón	Pants	Medias	Tights	Sandalias	Sandals
Pantalón corto	Shorts	Calcetines	Socks	Zapatos	Shoes
Sudadera	Hoodie	Pijama	Pajamas	Zapatillas	Sport shoes
Sueter	Sweater	Calzón	Underwear	Aretes	Earrings
Vestido	Dress	Gafas de sol	Sunglasses	Botas	Boots
Traje	Suit	Traje de baño	Swimsuit	Guantes	Gloves
Corbata	Tie	Abrigo	Coat	Gorro	Hat
Cinturón	Belt	Reloj	Watch	Collar	Necklace

LET'S PRACTICE!

The following are scrambled sentences with this new vocabulary.
Put the words in order and write the complete sentences below.

-camisa. una roja comprar Quiero

....

- es Ese bonito. muy azul abrigo un
- usa Patricio impermeable su llueve. cuando

....

-un verde ¿Tiene vestido 14? talla

....

-aretes Compré largos. unos

....

-sandalias Esas altas. muy son

....

-los de Me baño gustan trajes flores. con

....

Read this dialogue out loud about a husband buying clothes for his wife's birthday.

- Alfonso: ¡Hola! ¿Tiene ropa para mujeres?
- Vendedora: ¡Sí! Tenemos faldas, camisas, abrigos y vestidos. ¿Qué busca usted?
- Alfonso: Quiero comprar una falda verde, una camisa blanca, un abrigo azul y un vestido rosa para mi esposa. Es su cumpleaños.
- Vendedora: Bien. ¿Cuál es el talle de su esposa?
- Alfonso: Mi esposa tiene un talla 16.
- Vendedora: Bien. Ya busco todo.
- Vendedora: Aquí tiene todo.
- Alfonso: ¡Excelente! Quiero una bolsa para regalo.
- Vendedora: Ya lo preparo.
- Alfonso: ¿Cuánto es en total?
- Vendedora: Son 125 dólares. ¿Paga con tarjeta de crédito?
- Alfonso: No. Uso mi tarjeta de débito. Aquí está.
- Vendedora: Muy bien. Gracias por su compra señor.
- Alfonso: ¡Adiós!

LET'S PRACTICE!

Grammar Review

Answer these questions using the correct verb tense.

- ¿Adónde fuiste ayer?

_____

- ¿Qué compraste en la tienda?

_____

- ¿Cuántos años tienes?

_____

- ¿Cuándo es tu cumpleaños?

_____

- ¿Estudiaste español el sábado?

_____

- ¿Hay una lámpara en tu dormitorio?

_____

- ¿Qué hiciste la semana pasada?

_____

- ¿Quién es tu mejor amigo?
  _____

- ¿Prefieres leer o mirar la televisión?
  _____

- ¿Qué comiste para el desayuno?
  _____

- ¿Cómo llegas al supermercado?
  _____

- ¿Cuándo terminaste el trabajo?
  _____

- ¿De dónde eres?
  _____

- ¿Cómo eres?
  _____

- ¿Fuiste al parque esta semana?
  _____

Preposition Review

Fill in the blanks with the right preposition. Please choose from these prepositions-
cerca de, con, contra, de, debajo de, en, entre, encima, para, por, sobre. More than
one option is correct in many sentences. You can return to Chapter 16 if you need to
review it a little more.

- Tengo un lápiz _____ rosa.
- Los libros están _____ de la mesa.
- Yo pago por los productos del supermercado _____ tarjeta de crédito.
- La niña está _____ tú y yo.
- Nosotros estudiamos _____ una hora.
- Los zapatos están _____ de la mesa.
- Ella juega _____ su amiga.
- María habla _____ historia en la clase de español.
- Mi cocina está _____ la sala.
- Pablo puso las bolsas _____ la mesa.

CHAPTER 18

COMPARATIVES AND SUPERLATIVES

"Sale más caro el collar que el perro"- The collar costs more than the dog! Some of our favorite proverbs and expressions are based on comparatives and superlatives. Comparatives and superlatives are both adjectives. We use comparatives to compare equality or inequality between two nouns and superlatives to compare more than two nouns. Understanding how to compare in both cases will improve your speaking ability.

Comparing inequality nouns

This comparison indicates that one noun is more or less than the other. (Juan is taller than Camila/This painting is more beautiful than the picture/ Camila is shorter than Juan/ The picture is less beautiful than the painting) When we compare two things in English, we usually add "more" before the adjective or "er" onto its end.

In Spanish, it is even easier. If you need to express that one thing is MORE than the other, we use "más+adjective+que" and if you need to express that one thing is LESS than the other, we use "menos+adjective+que". It is really very simple! Let´s see some examples:

- Fernando corre más rápido que Teresa.
- El pastel de chocolate es más delicioso que la tarta de fresas.
- El café está más caliente que el helado.
- Este color celeste es menos intenso que el rojo.
- Este vestido es menos llamativo que la minifalda.
- Esta galleta es menos dulce que tu magdalena.

LET´S PRACTICE!

Write más or menos and que according to your opinion.

Maria y Julia son	más	bonitas	necklace	Daniela y Eva
El té y el café son		saludables		el vino y el whisky
El león está		hambriento		el caballo
El elefante es		pesado		el ratón
La luna está		cerca		el sol
El avión vuela		alto		el helicóptero
La música clásica es		agradable		el rock
Estas patatas están		saladas		la pizza

Write your own comparisons. Using the following nouns, adjectives, and verbs. You will need to modify the adjective according to the subject you choose.

For example: Ella es más simpática que tu prima Estela.

Yo	somos	simpático	yo
Tus amigos	soy	inteligente	tus amigos
Los niños	es	atlético	los niños
Ella	son	gracioso	ella
El Sr. Perez		trabajador	el Sr. Perez
Nosotras		ordenado	nosotras
Mis amigos y yo		activo	mis amigos y yo
Mi primo Carlos		tímido	tu prima Estela

....

....

....

....

....

....

....

Irregular comparatives adjectives

A few Spanish words don't use *más o menos* because they are irregular comparatives adjectives. Some of them are also irregular in English. In these cases, it is important just to remember the form:

Adjetivo	Adjective	Comparativo	Plural	Comparative
bueno	good	mejor	mejores	better
malo	bad	peor	peores	worse
grande	big	mayor	mayores	bigger
pequeño	small	menor	menores	smaller
viejo	old	mayor	mayores	older

Read out aloud the following example sentences.

- Mi hermano mayor es más alto que yo.
- La población de Estados Unidos es mayor que la de Jamaica.
- La pobreza es peor en África que en Asia.
- Esta comida es peor que la comida de ese restaurante.
- Mi amigo Alberto es menor que mi primo Jorge.
- El helado de vainilla está a menor temperatura que el chocolate caliente.
- El queso se conserva mejor en el refrigerador que fuera de él.
- Ver las obras de arte en el Museo es mejor que verlas en un libro.

LET'S PRACTICE!

Complete the following sentences using irregular comparative adjectives.

- Estas manzanas parecen _____ que aquellos plátanos verdes.
- Carolina cocina _____ que su mamá.
- Las hamburguesas son _____ que la comida de mi casa.
- Esas niñas son _____ que mis vecinas.
- Mi esposo es _____ que mi padre.
- Esta mesa está _____ que las sillas.

Comparing equality nouns

Another way is to compare two objects, people, things, etc. If you need to compare equality between two, you say "is so … as" (es+tan+adjective+como). If you need negative equality between two, you say … "is not as….as" (no+tan+adjective+como). Using the words of the above chart, we can say:

- Yo soy tan simpático como el Sr. Perez.
- Los niños no son tan tímidos como mis amigos y yo.
- Nosotras somos tan ordenadas como tus amigos.
- Ella no es tan graciosa como tu prima Estela.

Can you write five more sentences using these examples?

....

....

....

....

....

To conclude with this part of the chapter, think about comparisons in pairs:

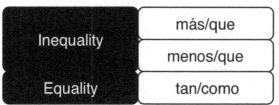

Inequality	más/que
	menos/que
Equality	tan/como

más/que
menos/que
tan/como

LET'S PRACTICE!

They can't match with a word that is outside their pair. Let's fill in the following blanks with either como or que. Look at the rest of the sentence to find the other half of the pair before deciding which one to put in the blank.

a. Mis amigos son tan jóvenes _____ mis primos.
b. Yo soy más débil _____ tú.
c. Nosotros somos menos fuertes _____ ellos.
d. Mi silla es tan roja _____ tu silla.
e. Mi hermana corre más rápido _____ Andrea.
f. El camión va más despacio _____ el tren.
g. Mi almuerzo no es tan abundante _____ el desayuno de Felipe.
h. La sandía no es tan dulce _____ el melón.
i. El Centro Comercial es más pequeño _____ el parque.
j. El Museo es menos popular _____ el Centro Comercial.

Comparing more than two nouns

We use superlatives to compare more than two nouns. A superlative adjective indicates that a noun has more or less of a special quality than the others. Most of the time in English, we use an *est* ending on the adjective- the tallest, the quickest, the smallest. Sometimes, we use *most or least* in front of the adjectives. In Spanish, we use the following formula:

definite article (el-la-los-las) + "más" (more) or "menos (less) + the adjective (quality to emphasize). So, to use a superlative adjective, we have to recognize the gender and number of the noun (feminine or masculine, singular or plural). Look at these examples:

- Pedro es el más inteligente de la clase.
- María es la más pequeña.
- Mi padre es el mayor de los hermanos.

- Mi madre es la mejor cocinera.
- Ese corredor es el más veloz de la carrera.
- Esta fruta es la más dulce.
- Este café es el más caliente.
- Este dormitorio es el más ordenado.

Some more adjectives

You already learned a lot of adjectives in chapter 4. Let´s review them putting them into practice. If you do not remember the meaning of a word, you can go back to look at the chart. Here are some new ones.

- Delgado- thin
- Suave- soft
- Estudioso- studious
- Perezoso- lazy
- Trabajadorr- hard-working
- Claro- light
- Bonito- beautiful
- Feo- ugly
- Cruel- cruel or mean
- Luminoso- brigh

LET´S PRACTICE!

Comparison Practice

Read out loud these sentences. Underline the comparative or superlative phrases.

Ella es más rápida que su maestro.

Las sillas de la sala son mejores que las sillas de la cocina.

La manzana es la mejor fruta.

Briana es la más inteligente de su clase.

Los tenedores están más limpios que las cucharas.

Marcos es tan estudioso como su amigo.

Mi hermano es tan perezoso como yo.

Las lámparas son menos viejas que las sábanas.

El comedor es más grande que la cocina.

El desayuno es mejor que el almuerzo.

Read about this person's home. After reading write some sentences about your home that compare it to this home. There are a few questions underneath the paragraph to get you started.

Yo vivo en una casa. No es una casa grande, pero es muy luminosa.
Solo tiene un piso. En mi casa hay un baño, un dormitorio y una cocina.
No tiene una sala. Tiene un comedor muy grande. En mi dormitorio,
tengo una cama y un escritorio. Yo trabajo en el escritorio. En la cocina,
hay dos sillas y una mesa pequeña. Mis dos tenedores, dos cucharas
y tres cuchillos están en la cocina. En el baño tengo una toalla.

You can answer these questions or start your paragraph about what is different or similar.

- ¿Cuántas toallas tienes?
- ¿Tu casa es más grande o más pequeña?
- ¿El comedor de tu casa es tan pequeño?
- ¿Tienes más muebles en tu dormitorio?
- ¿Es más o menos luminosa?

....
....
....
....
....

Comparison Review

Complete the missing words and complete this paragraph to describe one person. The options for the blanks are- *quince, más, menos, tan, amigo, escuela, guapo, música.*

Yo tengo un _____. Se llama Marcos. Marcos es _____ alto que yo.
Marcos tiene pelo rubio y tiene _____ años. Marcos es atlético. Yo
también soy atlético. Marcos es _____ atlético como yo. A Marcos le
gusta dibujar. A mí no me gusta dibujar. Yo soy _____ artístico que
Marcos. Nos gusta escuchar _____ juntos. Vamos a la misma
_____. Después de clase, vamos a comer. Marcos come mucha
comida. Yo no como tanto. Marcos paga la comida. Marcos es el
estudiante más _____ de toda la escuela.

CHAPTER 19

PRESENT CONTINUOUS TENSE

So many times, in English, we want to use the continuous tense when speaking about things we ARE DOING.

When learning Spanish, it's easier to learn simple present first, but if you prefer to say I AM RIDING, YOU ARE STUDYING, THEY ARE LISTENING, rather than I ride, you study, and they listen, now you will be able to do this. Just like in English, the present continuous verb form has two parts.

The verb forms the first part to be. (*Ser* and *estar*). When using the present continuous form, we will use estar. *Estar* is a verb used for more temporary things. If you ARE DOING something, that is temporary. The second part is the gerund of the verb. The gerund is the form of the verb that ends in ando (if the infinitive finishes with ar) or iendo (if the infinitive finishes with er or ir.

Let's review the conjugation of estar for the present continuous.

Yo	estoy	Nosotros	Estamos
Tú	estás	Vosotros	Estáis
Ella/él/usted	está	Ellos/ustedes	Estaron

This is the first part of the verb form, the "am, is, are," etc.

In the past tense chapter, we also talked about the root of *estar* in the past. However, we never really focused on it. Let's take a minute to review that conjugation as well, because if you can remember these two charts, you can do both present continuous and past continuous.

Yo	estuve	Nosotros	estuvimos
Tú	estuviste	Vosotros	estuvisteis
Ella/él/usted	estuvo	Ellos/ustedes	estuvieron

LET'S PRACTICE!

As a warmup practice, complete the correct tense and form of the following points:

- Yo/estar/ present _____
- Ellos/estar/ preterite _____
- Nosotros/estar/ present _____
- Tú/estar/ present _____
- Él/ estar/ preterite _____
- Ella/ estar/ present _____

Look above to check your work.

Forming the present participle

The present participle is the fancy way of identifying the "-ing" verb. With the present continuous form, we use "-ing" in English.

To form the gerund of an "ar" verb, take out the "ar", leave the stem and add "ando". Let´s see some examples:

Infinitive	Meaning	Stem (without ar)	Gerund (with ando)	Meaning
Trabajar	To work	Trabaj-	Trabajando	Working
Hablar	To talk	Habl-	Hablando	Talking
Jugar	To play	Jug-	Jugando	Playing
Cocinar	To cook	Cocin-	Cocinando	Cooking
Nadar	To swim	Nad-	Nadando	Swimming
Mirar	To look	Mir-	Mirando	Looking

Read aloud these sentences:

- Estoy cocinando.
- Ellos están nadando.
- Tú estás trabajando.
- Nosotros estamos jugando.

To form the gerund of an "er or ir" verb, take out the "er or ir", leave the stem and add "iendo". Let´s see some examples:

Infinitive	Meaning	Stem (without ar)	Gerund (with ando)	Meaning
Beber	To drink	Beb-	Bebiendo	Drinking
Comer	To eat	Com-	Comiendo	Eating
Vivir	To live	Viv-	Viviendo	Living
Partir	To leave	Part-	Partiendo	Leaving
Romper	To break	Romp-	Rompiendo	Breaking
Escribir	To write	Escrib-	Escribiendo	Writing

Read aloud these sentences:

- Nosotros estamos escribiendo.
- Ellos están partiendo.
- Tú estás bebiendo.
- Nosotros estamos comiendo.

Write the gerund of these verbs in parenthesis in order to build correct sentences:

- Estamos _____(jugar) tenis en el parque.
- Carolina está _____(cantar) con Rafael.
- Martín y yo estamos _____(mirar) una película de suspenso.
- Mi mamá está _____(cocinar) un pastel de manzanas.
- Federico está _____(caminar) por el Centro Comercial.
- Nosotros estamos _____(subir) las escaleras.
- Tomás está _____(bailar) tango con Mercedes.
- Mariano y Enrique están _____(hablar) sobre sus viajes.
- Mis vecinos están _____(reparar) la puerta de su casa ahora.
- Andrés está _____(escribir) una novela romántica.
- Yo estoy _____(trabajar) con Esteban en el proyecto.

The exception

Of course, there is an exception. If the root of the word, once you have taken off that *-ar, -er, -ir* ending, it finishes with a vowel, then you will use '-yendo' as your ending.

Let's look at an example of this.
- Leer- to read
- Yo estoy leyendo. - I am reading.
- Ellos están leyendo. - They are reading.

When we take off the 'er' of the verb 'leer,' we are left with le-. Because that last letter is a vowel, we need '-yendo' instead of '-iendo.' Here's another example.

- Creer- to believe. Ellos están creyendo.
- Caer –to fall down. Nosotros estamos cayendo.

All verbs ending with *-uir* add *-yendo*. For example: *construir, huir,* etc. There aren't very many verbs in Spanish that have this vowel ending on the root, but when you see one, just remember the difference in ending.

- Construir- to build. Él está construyendo.
- Excluir –to exclude. Ella está excluyendo.

Negative Sentences

Just like with the verb tenses, negative sentences are very simple. You just add a 'no' right before the conjugated verb or BOTH parts of the verb phrase. Don't interrupt the verb phrase by putting no in the middle. Here are some examples.

- El perro no está ladrando.
- Los niños no están estudiando.
- Yo no estoy jugando al béisbol.

LET'S PRACTICE!

Write the negative sentence of the following ones:

- María está manejando ahora.
- ....

- Juana estudia todos los días.
- ....

- Tú y tus amigos juegan fútbol en el parque.
- ....

- Martín trabaja mucho en su computadora.
- ....

- Nosotros estamos hablando sobre la fiesta de ayer.
- ....

- Yo hablo inglés.
- ....

- Nosotros cantamos mucho.
- ....

- Mis amigos están escribiendo en sus cuadernos.
- ....

- El gato está haciendo mucho ruido.
- ....

- Tú estás leyendo un libro de aventuras.
- ....

CHAPTER 20

SIMPLE FUTURE TENSE

The future tense expresses an intention of acting in the future. There are different ways to conjugate the verbs in the future and this chapter, will focus on the Simple Future.

Future verb tense conjugation

In English, we simply stick "will" before a verb and call it future tense. It works in another way in Spanish but all verbs (*-ar, -er, and -ir*) use the same conjugation for the future, so that should make it just a little bit simpler. To build the Simple Future tense, just add the following endings to the infinitive verb (no matter if it finishes with are, er or ir).

Persona	Final	Caminar	Beber	Vivir
Yo	é	caminaré	beberé	viviré
Tú	ás	caminarás	beberás	vivirás
Él/ella/usted	á	caminará	beberá	vivirá
Nosotros/as	emos	caminaremos	beberemos	viviremos
Vosotros	éis	caminaréis	beberéis	viviréis
Ellos/ellas/ustedes	án	caminarán	beberán	vivirán

Here is an example.
- I will work-
- Yo trabajaré

There are two details to observe. To build the future tense, we do not take off the 'ar, er or ir' endings before adding on é. The other point is that the form nosotros/nosotras is the only one with no accent. The acentos are important to pronounce the words properly. Read a couple more examples, then try it for yourself.

- They will add
- Ellos añadirán

- You will try
- Tú tratarás

- She will ask
- Ella preguntará

Turn each of the following sentences in present tense into future tense.

- Yo bebo _____
- Ellos venden _____
- Nosotros hablamos _____
- Tú descansas _____
- Él comparte _____
- Mis padres abren _____
- Usted monta _____
- Vosotros limpiáis _____
- Yo corro _____
- Nosotros enseñamos _____

Irregular future verb tense

In this verb tense, some verbs are irregular. The verbs PONER, SALIR, VENIR, VALER AND TENER ARE IRREGULAR. The vowel of the endings of the verbs in the infinitive must become a D. The 'd' replaces the 'e' or 'i' in the ending. Five verbs follow this *rule- tener, poner, salir, valer,* and *venir.* Let's review the meaning of all of those verbs.

- Tener- to have
- Poner- to put
- Salir- to go out or to exit
- Valer- to be worth
- Venir- to come

Tener becomes "tendr-" before adding on the future tense ending. If you want to say I will have, you would add the future tense ending for *yo* onto the end of "tendr."

- Yo tendré. I will have.
- Yo tendré una reunión mañana. I will have a meeting tomorrow.

- Pondremos los zapatos debajo de la mesa. We will put the shoes under the table.
- Saldrá más tarde que yo. He/she will go out later than me.

Change the root

Decir and *hacer* drop the 'ce' and 'ec' completely, so the root becomes

- Decir- dir-
- Hacer- har-

- Yo diré la verdad mañana- I will tell the truth tomorrow.
- Ellos harán su trabajo más tarde- They will do their work later.

Drop the "E"

Last, a group of verbs drop the 'e' before the r. The verbs that follow this rule are *haber, caber, poder, querer, saber*. We have reviewed three of these five verbs, though you may also recognize the fourth.

- Haber- This is the verb that becomes hay (there is, there are).
- Caber- to fit
- Poder- to be able to
- Querer- to want
- Saber- to know

Check out these examples, then we'll do a little practice with the irregulars.

- Querré estudiar más. I will want to study more.
- Habrá quince estudiantes. There will be fifteen students.
- Podrán manejar a mi casa. They will be able to drive to my house.
- Sabrás la decisión correcta en el momento. You'll know the right decision at the time.
- El libro cabrá en la mochila. The book will fit in the backpack.

Irregular verbs practice

Read aloud the following sentences:

1. Yo diré la verdad.   _____
2. Ellos querrán jugar con los niños.   _____
3. Podremos salir a las nueve.   _____
4. Tendrás veinte estudiantes.   _____
5. Saldré más tarde.   _____

I am going to….

There is another way to discusse future, including a verb we have already learned- *ir*. It allows us to express the present statement with a sense of the future. It is often used instead of the Future Simple tense to express something that will happen soon or a planned action shortly. *Ir* means to go. It has an irregular conjugation:

Yo	voy	Nosotros	vamos
Tú	vas	Vosotros	vais
Ella/él/usted	va	Ellos/ustedes	van

One way we can say things in the future in English is to say "I am going to ____." For example,

- I am going to study.
- He is going to listen.

We can follow the same format in Spanish. The verb to go (ir) is the only one that needs to be modified according to the person (subject) of the action. Use this formula to make your sentences.

Conjugated ir + a + infinite verb

- Yo voy a manejar. I am going to drive.
- Tú vas a preguntar. You are going to ask.

LET'S PRACTICE!

Fill in the blanks with the correctly conjugated *ir* for each of the following sentences.

1. Nosotros _____ a practicar fútbol.
2. Ellos _____ a tratar de aprender el español.
3. Yo _____ a cambiar las luces.
4. Ella ____ a llamar a su amigo.
5. Tú _____ a jugar tenis con Marcela.
6. Usted _____a trabajar mañana.
7. Ustedes _____a cantar en la fiesta.
8. Yo _____ a saltar mucho.
9. Ellas _____a jugar a las cartas.
10. Nosotras _____a hacer compras.

As long as we know the conjugation for ir, this is a pretty simple form.
I WILL or I'm going to? We can use both forms. It's really up to personal choice. It's good to understand the endings and functions, though, so that we will understand what someone else may be saying. I WILL versus I'm going to or I'm planning to.

Complete these exercises.
Read the following conversation out loud. Then, answer the questions below.

Antonio: ¿Qué vas a hacer este fin de semana?
José: Yo voy a estudiar mucho. Tengo un examen el lunes.
Antonio: ¿Para qué clase es tu examen?
José: Es para español. Quiero salir con mis amigos, pero me quedaré estudiando.
Antonio: Yo voy a la casa de mis abuelos. Mis abuelos me llevarán al Restaurante La Parolaccia.
José: Mmmm, ¡que rico!

1. ¿Qué hará José este fin de semana?

_____

2. ¿Por qué va a estudiar?

_____

3. ¿A qué restaurante irá Antonio?

_____

Let's work with another conversation.
Read aloud this conversation and answer the questions.

Juan: Hoy es el último día de escuela. ¿Qué harás durante las vacaciones de verano?
Tomás: No sé. Quiero ir a la playa, pero mis hermanos quieren ir a las montañas. Creo que iremos a acampar.
Juan: ¿Te gusta acampar?
Tomás: No mucho. Yo prefiero leer un libro o escuchar música en la playa. ¿Qué planes tienes tú?
Juan: Yo voy a volar a Italia y pasaré junio allá. Luego, voy a Canadá por un mes. Dibujaré mucho y no tendré que hacer nada de libros ni estudios.
Tomás: ¡Suena bien divertido!
Juan: ¿Vas a venir conmigo?
Tomás: Quiero, pero no puedo.

1. ¿Adónde va Juan en sus vacaciones?

_____

2. ¿En qué se diferencia Tomás de sus hermanos?

_____

3. ¿Qué quiere hacer Tomás?

_____

In this practice, you must fill in the blank with the verb in the correct future tense. Sometimes, you will need to use the "will" future form, and others need to use the "going" future form.

1. Mario y yo _____ un pastel para el cumpleaños de mi mamá. (hacer)
2. Beatriz _____ a _____ en una oficina nueva. (trabajar)
3. Martina, ¿_____a ir a la fiesta mañana? (ir)
4. Mis amigos _____a ganar mil dólares. (ganar)
5. Manolo _____ todo del horario. (recordar)
6. Manuel y Carlos _____a nadar en la laguna. (nadar)
7. Victoria y Teresa_____ a sus padres el mes que viene (visitar)
8. Marcelo _____a comprar papas y hamburguesas. (comprar)
9. Camilo, ¿_____esa porción de pizza? (comer)
10. Yo _____ en helicóptero por la ciudad de Nueva York. (volar)
11. Tú _____una maratón de 10 millas. (correr)
12. Miranda _____a comprar un libro de cuentos infantil. (comprar)
13. Nosotras_____a limpiar la casa mañana. (limpiar)
14. Nosotras no _____de vacaciones en febrero. (estar)
15. No _____a trabajar el próximo sábado. (trabajar)

Let's do one more practice!
Read the sentence in one form of the future tense and change it to the other.

1. Ellos estudiarán por tres horas. _____
2. Nosotros diremos la verdad. _____
3. Yo me dormiré muy tarde. _____
4. Tú llevarás un vestido bonito. _____
5. Bárbara va a estudiar. _____
6. Mis amigos van a llamar a la maestra. _____
7. Tú no vas a esperar mucho tiempo. _____

CHAPTER 21

MASTERING THE VERBS

LET'S PRACTICE!
Which tense is it?

Identify the tense of the following verbs. Remember their meaning and the subject pronoun (yo, tú, él, ella, usted, nosotros, ellos, ustedes) as well.

1. Estoy trabajando.
2. Yo bebo.
3. Ellas practican.
4. Ellos practicaron.
5. Camila va a estudiar.
6. Yo no trabajé.
7. Nosotros enseñamos.
8. Miguel habló.
9. Yo no montaré ese caballo.
10. Tú no estás limpiando.

Fill in the blanks

Choose one of the following verbs off the list to complete the following paragraphs. First, read the verbs and find each meaning. Then read the paragraph to discover which verb is missing in each blank. You must select the verb that makes sense for each sentence and change the ending to the correct tense.

Using the past tense: vivir, asignar, ser, hablar, vender, llevar, trabajar

Hace tres años, yo _____ en una casa grande. Había tres dormitorios, pero el sofá de la sala _____ siempre mi lugar preferido para descansar. Una mañana, mi carro se descompuso, entonces un amigo vino a casa y me _____ al trabajo. Llegué muy tarde y mi jefe (boss) me _____ muchas tareas. No me gustó trabajar tanto. Después de un año, yo _____ la casa y me mudé a un apartamento.

Using the two options to conjugate a verb in the future tense: volver, cambiar, hacer, vivir, esperar, llamar, dormir, jugar, ir

Después de la escuela, yo _____ a la universidad. _____ en mi nuevo apartamento desde agosto y _____ hasta que empiecen las clases. Yo _____ muchos amigos y nosotros _____ fútbol después de clase. Mi mamá me _____ muchas veces para hablar conmigo. Yo me _____ muy tarde en la noche y tú _____ tu horario para tener clases conmigo.

Write your own sentences

Write your own sentences with each of the following words. After the space, a sample sentence has been provided. (Example sentences)

Voy /_____
Yo voy a escribir una carta a mi madre.

Sin /_____
No quiero comer sin agua.

También /_____
Ellos también quieren venir.

Dos/_____
Hay dos puertas en mi salón de clase.

Estás/_____
Tú estás manejando muy rápido.

Menos /_____
Yo soy menos inteligente que él.

Entre /_____
Mi escritorio está entre las lámparas.

Debajo de /_____
Yo busco mi lápiz debajo del sofá.

Fueron /_____
Mis amigos fueron a la escuela a las nueve y media.

Izquierda /_____
La gasolinera está a la izquierda de la biblioteca.

Now, write some questions using the following words. Once again, sample questions have been provided for you.

¿Qué? _____
¿Qué estás haciendo?

¿Dónde? _____
¿Dónde está tu casa?

¿Quién? _____
¿Quién es tu mejor amigo?

¿Cuál? _____
¿Cuál es tu comida favorita?

¿Cuándo? _____
¿Cuándo es tu clase de español?

Reading practice

Story 1

Read the following story and find all the verbs. Focus on their meanings and identify their tenses (present, past, future, present progressive). Then, answer the questions about the story. Find enough verbs to fill in all the blanks.

Hay una niña que se llama Gabriela. Gabriela vive en Costa Rica y tiene cinco mascotas. Dos de las mascotas son perros. Los perros juegan y corren rápido. Un perro es blanco tiene manchas negras y el otro es gris.

Además ella tiene dos tortugas. Las tortugas son muy lentas y comen zanahorias, manzanas y lechugas pero muy despacio. Gabriela recibirá otra tortuga para cuidar en una semana.

Por último, ella tiene un gato. El gato duerme al sol sobre un almohadón verde. A veces se acerca a los perros y otras se esconde.

Gabriela cuida a los animales con gran responsabilidad.

Now, answer these questions.

1. ¿Cuántas mascotas tiene Gabriela?

2. ¿Cuáles son las mascotas?

3. ¿Cómo son los perros?

4. ¿Qué animal recibirá Gabriela?

That story was mostly in the present tense and told you about someone (rather than events that happened).

Story 2

Go ahead and read this second story which follows a typical story pattern. Once again, identify the verbs and find their meanings before answering questions.

Pablo estudió mucho para su examen de inglés durante todo el día. Su madre entró en su dormitorio.

—Pablo, ¿qué haces? —le preguntó su madre.

—Estudio, Mamá. Necesito aprobar el examen.

—Bueno, la cena está lista. Puedes comer con nosotros.

Pablo bajó por las escaleras hacia la cocina y comió una cena deliciosa. Su mamá hizo puré de papas y pollo, la cena favorita de Pablo.

—Gracias, mamá. Está muy rico.

-Ahora, vas a estudiar otra vez.

Pablo llevó su libro a la sala y estudió allí. Leyó un largo rato hasta que su hermana entró y le habló.

—Pablo, ¿qué haces?

—¡Estudio! —gritó Pablo.

—Quiero jugar contigo.

—No, no puedo jugar. Estudiaré en mi dormitorio —dijo Pablo y regresó a su dormitorio otra vez.

What verbs did you find? Complete the table with ten verbs of the dialogue and their tenses.

	Verb	Tense
1		
2		
3		
4		
5		
6		
7		
8		
9		
10		

Now, answer these questions.

1. ¿Qué está haciendo Pablo?
_____

2. ¿Dónde estudia?
_____

3. ¿Por qué estudia?
_____

4. ¿Qué comió Pablo?
_____

CHAPTER 22

BODY PARTS AND HEALTH VOCABULARY

Body Parts

We will start with some basic body parts (partes del cuerpo) before moving into other useful vocabulary and phrases. We have broken these parts into words.

Head / Cabeza				
	Eye	Ojo	Eyelid	Párpado
	Eyelashes	Pestañas	Eyebrows	Cejas
	Ear	Oído (inside)	Ear	Oreja (outside)
	Nose	Nariz	Mouth	Boca
	Jaw	Mandíbula	Lips	Labios
	Tongue	Lengua	Teeth	Diente
	Throat	Garganta	Forehead	Frente
	Cheek	Mejilla	Beard	Barba
	Hair	Pelo	Chin	Barbilla
	Freckles	Pecas	Neck	Cuello
	Brain	Cerebro	Skull	Craneo
	Face	Cara	Nape	Nuca

Torso / Torso				
	Chest	Pecho	Back	Espalda
	Heart	Corazón	Lungs	Pulmones
	Muscle	Músculo	Skin	Piel
	Waist	Cintura	Stomach	Estómago
	Abs	Abdominales	Navel	Ombligo
	Breast	Pecho	Organs	Órganos
	Intestines	Intestinos	Kidney	Riñones
	Liver	Hígado	Bone	Hueso
	Ribs	Costillas	Skeleton	Esqueleto
	Spine	Columna	Blood	Sangre
	Testicle	Testículo	Spleen	Bazo
	Veins	Venas	Ovary	Ovario
	Shoulders	Hombros	Tummy	Barriga

Arm / Brazo				
	Elbow	Codo	Forearm	Antebrazo
	Wrist	Muñeca	Hand	Mano
	Palm	Palma	Finger	Dedo
	Thumb	Pulgar	Fingertips	Puntas de los dedos
	Fingernails	Uñas	Fingerprints	Huellas

Leg pierna	hip	cadera	butt	Culo
	thigh	muslo	knee	Rodilla
	calf	pantorrilla	ankle	Tobillo
	foot	pie	heel	Talón
	toe	Dedo del pie	buttocks	nalgas

LET'S PRACTICE!

These are the basic body parts.
Before we add in some phrases let's practice! Find these words.

NARIZ	BOCA	LENGUA	OREJA	PELO	NUCA	OMBLIGO
HOMBRO	ESPALDA	TORSO	FRENTE	MEJILLA	PIERNA	CODO
MANO	DEDO	ESTOMAGO	NALGA	TOBILLO	DIENTE	PECHO
	CINTURA	RODILLA	VENAS	MUSCULO	LABIOS	

```
J  M  Y  E  Y  F  M  U  S  C  U  L  O  X
V  J  I  D  V  R  Y  E  X  O  O  J  C  Q
L  T  C  K  E  E  H  S  W  D  S  X  I  Y
E  B  O  F  N  N  O  T  V  O  G  W  N  O
N  P  D  R  A  T  M  O  R  E  J  A  T  M
G  E  R  I  S  E  B  M  X  F  P  A  U  B
U  L  O  P  E  O  R  A  N  R  E  X  R  L
A  O  D  I  R  N  O  G  A  Q  C  D  A  I
Y  C  I  E  T  A  T  O  R  H  H  E  M  G
B  J  L  R  Q  L  B  E  I  R  O  D  A  O
M  B  L  N  Q  G  O  V  Z  O  N  O  N  R
S  Z  A  A  E  A  C  J  O  J  G  U  O  K
M  E  J  I  L  L  A  B  I  O  S  O  C  G
E  S  P  A  L  D  A  V  J  S  P  I  V  A
```

Use the blank space below to put your best artistic skills to use. Draw a picture of a person (stick figures work just fine) and label their body parts.

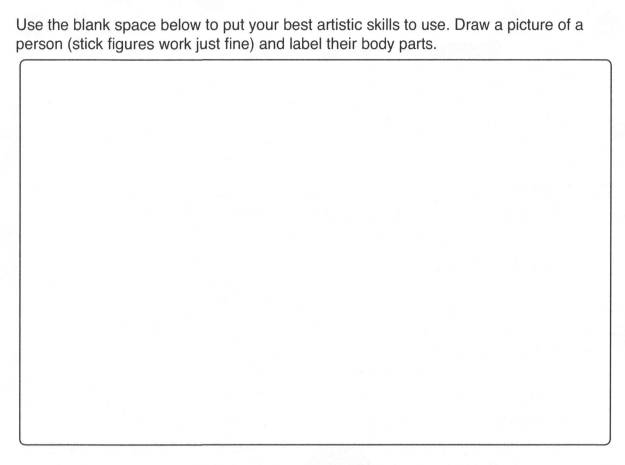

If we get hurt or start to feel pain somewhere, we need to be able to communicate what is going on so that the doctor can get us the proper help. With many injuries, we can point to the body part, and the doctor should be able to figure out what is hurting. However, it doesn't hurt to be able to explain what you are feeling, how long you have been feeling it, and anything else relevant.

Remember that we already know right (*derecho/a*) and left (*izquierdo/a*), and we can use that to identify *which shoulder*, ear, or whatever is hurting.

More vocabulary (Injuries)

- Inflamada- swollen (note that this is an adjective, so it can become male or female based on what body part you are describing. *Mi brazo está inflamado o mi pierna está inflamada.)*
- Dolorida- in pain/sore
- Urgente- pronounced like or-hen-tay, it means urgent
- La quemadura- The burn
- La fiebre- The fever
- La nariz tapada- The stuffy nose
- La tos- The cough
- El dolor- The pain
- El calambre- The cramp
- La alergia- The allergy
- La herida- The injury

- El enfermero- nurse
- El doctor- doctor
- La cirugia- surgery
- El medicamento- medicine
- La pastilla- pill
- El tratamiento- treatment
- Enfermo- sick (this is an adjective, so remember it can be male or female)
- El accidente- accident

LET'S PRACTICE!

Read the following sentences out loud. Connect with lines their meanings

Tuve un accidente •	• I am sick
Tengo fiebre •	• I have pain in my back.
Usted necesita cirugía de rodilla •	• I had an accident
Estoy enfermo •	• You need knee surgery
Necesito atención urgente •	• I have allergies to peanut
Tengo una herida en mi pierna •	• My throat is swollen
Tengo dolor de espalda •	• I have a fever
Me duele el estómago •	• I did not drink a lot of water
No bebí mucha agua •	• Brush your teeth
Mi garganta está inflamada •	• I need urgent attention
Tengo alergias a los cacahuates •	• I have an injury in my leg.
Cepilla tus dientes •	• My stomach hurts

Conjugating and using *Doler*

The verb *doler* in Spanish means to hurt as in 'something hurts me' or 'something aches,' not as in 'I am hurting something else.' It has an irregular verbal conjugation and is pronominal or reflexive. As the verb *gustar* that we learned in Chapter 12, the pronominal or reflexive verbs refer to an action the subject carries out on himself. Other verbs like this are peinar (to comb), poner (to put on), sentar (to sit down) and despertar (to wake up). They are always conjugated with a reflexive pronoun that agrees with the number and person of the subject. This means that doler can be reflexively conjugated as dolerme, dolerte, dolerse, dolernos, doleros and dolerse.

First, the verb doler had a spelling change when conjugated in the present tense. Instead of the 'o' in the root of the word, you will have a 'ue.' The most common forms for this verb are:
- Duele
- Duelen

Let´s see some examples:

-Me duele la rodilla.
- ¿Te duele el estómago?
-Les duele la cabeza.
- A Nicolás le duele el tobillo.
-Me duele el oído.
-Nos duelen las piernas.
-Me duele el codo.
-Me duele el pie izquierdo.
-Les duelen las manos.

LET´S PRACTICE!

Let's make some sentences now. Remember to start with the person it hurts first.

- Make a sentence about your nose hurting you.

_____

- Make a sentence about your friend's finger hurting.

_____

- Make a sentence about both of your arms hurting.

_____

As mentioned above, this verb follows the same pattern as gustar. Let's practice what you already know.

Read these sentences out loud to find out what different people like.

- Me gusta jugar al béisbol.
- Nos gustan las galletas.
- Le gusta escuchar música.
- Les gusta ir a la tienda.

Practicing Medical Vocabulary

Read this sample conversation and answer the questions. Note that the doctor speaks to the patient with a more formal tone, so she uses usted. Then, respond to the doctor's questions in a similar conversation.

A: Hola, me llamo Doctora Inez. ¿Cómo se llama?
B: Me llamo Martín.
A: ¿Por qué está usted aquí hoy?

B: Me duele la espalda.
A: ¿Hace cuánto le duele?
B: Me duele desde hace dos días.
A: ¿Hizo usted algún tipo de ejercicio?
B: No, no hago ejercicio.
A: ¿Le duele siempre o solo a veces?
B: Siempre.
A: Okay, voy a tocar su espalda. Dígame si siente dolor.

LET´S PRACTICE!

1. ¿Qué parte del cuerpo le duele?

_____

2. ¿Cuánto tiempo hace que le duele la espalda?

_____

Let's pretend that your finger hurts.
Answer the following questions that a doctor might ask you about it.

1. ¿Qué le duele?

_____

2. ¿De la mano izquierda o derecha?

_____

3. En una escala de uno a diez, ¿cuánto le duele?

_____

4. ¿Tuvo un accidente?

_____

5. ¿Usted puede mover el dedo?

_____

6. ¿Usted tomó pastillas para el dolor?

_____

Identify the following vocabulary words. Try not to look back as you answer.

1. Fiebre _____
2. Corazón _____
3. Gusta _____
4. Me duele el ojo _____
5. Enfermo _____

CHAPTER 23

BOOSTING YOUR SPANISH WITH READING AND LISTENING

Learning a language is not something you can do for a few weeks then forever remember what you have studied. You must practice regularly. A word can't just be repeated senselessly. It needs to be used in context over some time. Aim to use each new word in a variety of different ways. Don't just read, you also need to listen and speak to make sure that your knowledge nests in your brain to be remembered forever.

Improving your reading skills

Before we get to the reading passages, let's review a few things you can do to ensure you gett out of your foreign language reading practice.

First, make sure you are reading something that interests you. While you can't pick the passages included for practice in this book, you can certainly look for other practice reading passages on topics that you enjoy. The more you enjoy, the more your brain will retain. Pick something easy to read.

Attempt to read a full chapter or several pages at a time. You may feel overwhelmed if you just read a paragraph and focus on the words you don't know.

When you get to words you don't know, use context clues like when you were learning to read English. Figure out the words around it and take a guess. You just might surprise yourself!

There are many more conjugations with verbs than the ones we have learned. You might see "hablaría" and not be sure exactly what that ending means. However, you know the verb "hablar." Plug it into the sentence even if you don't know exactly what version or verb tense it is. Usually, your brain can figure it out or get close enough that you know what the passage is saying.

DO NOT STOP FOR EVERY WORD! If you stop for every word you don't know, you won't get much anywhere. Pick a few random words that you don't recognize. Look those up and add them to a piece ofr easy reference. However, don't look up every word laboriously. Focus on trying to follow the story's main events.

Improving your listening skills

There are many ways to improve your listening skills, and it is often the part of language learning that is most easily neglected. However, you have many daily opportunities to turn on short stories or even just music in Spanish- when you are driving, cleaning, walking, or exercising.

If you have a friend who speaks Spanish, they would be the obvious choice for a speaking partner. However, if you don't, that doesn't mean that you can't do anything to improve.

You can

1. Switch all your devices to Spanish- your phone, tablet, and computer. Most of the clicks and navigations you do daily follow the same route, and you don't even read what you are clicking. However, if you put it in Spanish, you will get exposure to some new phrases and words.

2. Ask questions when listening. If you find someone who speaks Spanish, maybe not someone you meet with often, but just someone you see at the store, ask questions. Listening passively isn't enough. You want to engage with this person and learn as much as possible.

3. Keep a notebook with new vocabulary. Because Spanish easily connects how a word is said and how it is written, you can write down new words you learn while listening and review these words often.

4. Watch TV/movies in Spanish. If you have the option, slow the playback speed so they speak more slowly. Just like reading, don't focus on understanding every word. Just try to pick out the ones you recognize. You can put on Spanish subtitles if you want, but be aware that the subtitles don't always match the spoken words! Pick children's programs that are easy to follow even if you don't understand everything or a show that you already know well. Don't worry if it takes a while to adjust to hearing your favorite characters with a different voice actor or when their mouth doesn't match the words they are saying. However, this will help attune your ear to different accents.

Finally, enjoy every moment of your learning process. You are always improving your skills and climbing the mountain of Spanish knowledge. The higher you climb, the better the view!

CHAPTER 24

ADDITIONAL VOCABULARY AND ESSENTIAL PHRASES

Language is the main mean of communications for people. Thanks to it, we can exchange thoughts and feelings and knowing extra vocabulary words when you are learning a new language is essential for reading comprehension too. The more you learn, the better it will be for mastering your knowledge.

These lists include additional vocabulary you may need for your activities.

Computing/Informática

Arrastrar	To drag	Buscar	To search
Comenzar la sesión	To log in	Contraseña	Password
Disco duro	Hard disc	En línea	Online
Grabar/guardar	To save	La impresora	Printer
El teclado	The keyboard	Terminar la sesión	To log off
Página inicial	Homepage	Subir archivos	To upload files
Descargar	To download	Borrar/eliminar	To delete

Sports and hobbies/Deportes y pasatiempos

Artes marciales	Martial arts	Jugar a las damas	To play checkers
Astronomía	Astronomy	Patinaje	Skating
Ballet	Ballet	Ciclismo	Biking
Boxeo	Boxing	La jardinería	Gardening
Fotografía	Photography	Cocinar	Cooking
Gimnasia	Gymnastics	Navegar	Sailing
Jugar a las cartas	To play cards	Béisbol	Baseball
Boxear	Boxing	Trotar	Jogging
Nadar	Swimming	Pescar	Fishing
Acampar	Camping	Cuidar mascotas	Take care of pets
Leer	Reading	Carpintería	Carpentry
Jugar ajedrez	To play chess	Esquiar	Ski

Movies or theater/Películas o teatro

El actor	The actor	La actriz	The actress
Actuar	To act	aplaudir	To clap
El vestuario	Costume	La butaca	Box seat
La pantalla	The screen	El telón	Curtain
El espectáculo	Performance	La escenografía	Set design
El maquillaje	Makeup	Luces y sonido	Lights and sound
La estrella	Star	El escenario	Stage

Animals/animals

El ave	Bird	El canguro	Kangaroo
La cebra	Zebra	El cocodrilo	The crocodile
El delfin	The dolphin	La ballena	Whale
La araña	Spider	La hormiga	Ant
El ratón	Mice	La vaca	Cow
El caballo	Horse	La cabra	Goat
El conejo	Rabbit	El pavo	Turkey
La paloma	Dove	El venado	Deer
El buey	Ox	El cisne	Swan
El pato	Duck	La oveja	Sheep
La abeja	Bee	El loro	Parrot
El elefante	Elephant	El gorila	Gorilla
El mono	Monkey	La jirafa	Giraffe
El león	Lion	El oso	Bear
El perro	Dog	El gato	Cat
El pingüino	Penguin	La serpiente	Snake

Musical instruments/Instrumentos musicales

El acordeón	Accordion	El arpa	Harp
La armónica	Harmonica	El bajo	Bass
La batería	Drum set	El clarinete	Clarinet
La flauta dulce	Recorder	La flauta traversa	Flute
La guitarra	Guitar	La mandolina	Mandolin
El oboe	Oboe	El saxofón	Saxophone
El tambor	Drum	La trompeta	Trumpet
El trombón	Trombone	El piano	Piano
El violón	Violin	El violonchelo	Cello
El bajo	Bass guitar	La caja	Snare drum

False friends

A false friend is a word that looks like an English word, one you think you can guess what it means. However, it's nothing similar to the Spanish word. Below is a list of false friends in Spanish. Studying these is important so you don't make a silly mistake.

- Americano- a person from North or South America. We often use American to mean someone from the United States, but America stretches from the top of Canada down to the tip of Chile.
- Asistir- to attend, to be present. We might take it to mean helping someone, but if you want to talk about helping, you can use "ayudar."
- Bombero- firefighter. It has nothing to do with bombs!
- Carpeta- folder. Please don't walk on the carpeta because it's for sensitive documents.
- Casualidad- chance, opportunity. *De casualidad, vi a mi mejor amigo en el restaurante.*
- Chocar- to have an accident or to bump into.
- Colegio- high school (in Latin America, high school is 7th through 11th grade, and you graduate after that) *Universidad is college.*
- Compromiso- promise, commitment (engaged). It has nothing to do with coming to an agreement or a compromise.
- Delito- crime. You might think it sounds or looks like delight, but crimes are no delight.
- Disgusto- annoyance. It looks like *disgusting*, but has more to do with something you don't like.
- Embarazada- pregnant. If you want to say embarrassed, you would say *avergonzada*
- Enviar- to send. This has nothing to do with the emotion- of envy.
- Éxito - success. Voy a tener éxito con este libro.
- Fábrica- factory. While it could be *una fabrica de tela* (fabric factory), it could also be another type of factory.
- Lectura- reading, not a lecture. This is a noun. Yo practiqué lectura ayer.
- Molestar- to annoy. This has nothing to do with anything inappropriate. Yo molesté a mis amigos con mis bromas.
- Nudo- knot. Yo até un nudo con el mantel.
- Recordar- to remember. If you want to talk about recording something, you would say "grabar." Think of it like you are grabbing those few seconds of voice forever.
- Ropa- clothing. This is a noun that is always singular. For example, "No llevé mucha ropa a la playa."
- Sano- healthy, as far as the body goes. It has nothing to do with a mental state of health.
- Sopa- soup. Please don't talk about cleaning your body with *sopa* or you will get some funny looks.
- Vaso- glass for drinking. While you could put flowers here, you would most likely put them in a *jarrón* instead.

Review these important phrases

Review these questions/phrases and their meanings. Some of them will be used in the conversation exercise below. Answer the questions with as much detail as you can.

¿Qué te gusta hacer?	What do you like to do?
¿Cuántos años tienes?	How old are you?
¿Dónde trabaja usted?	Where do you work?
De nada.	You're welcome
Disculpe.	Excuse me
¿Cuánto cuesta?	How much does it cost?
¿Me puede traer _____?	Can you bring me _____?
¿Adónde le gustaría ir?	Where would you like to go?
¿Tiene hijos?	Do you have children?
La cuenta, por favor.	The bill, please
No hablo mucho español.	I don't speak much Spanish
Mucho gusto.	Nice to meet you
¿Cómo llego allí?	How do I get there?
Soy alérgica (o) a _____	I am allergic to _____
¿Cómo se dice _____ en español?	How do you say _____ in Spanish?
Ten cuidado.	Be careful
No sé dónde está_____.	I don't know where _____ is.
¿Qué recomiendas?	What do you recommend?
Yo necesito _____.	I need _____.
Me duele _____	My _____ hurts.

Proverbs/refranes

Let´s enjoy this last part. Un refrán is a phrase of popular origin traditionally repeated invariably, in which a moral thought, advice or teaching is expressed; particularly the one that is structured in verse and rhymes in assonance or consonance.

Más vale pájaro en mano que cien volando	A bird in the hand is worth two in the bush.
Quien primero viene, primero tiene	The early bird catches the worm
A buen entendedor, pocas palabras	A word to the wise
Más vale prevenir que curar	Better safe than sorry
Más vale tarde que nunca	Better late than never
Querer es poder	Where there is a will, there is a way
No todo lo que brilla es oro	All that glitters is not gold
Ojos que no ven, corazón que no siente	Out of sight, out of mind
En boca cerrada no entran moscas	Loose lips sink ships
Dime con quién andas y te diré quien eres	Birds of a feather flock together
El hábito no hace al monje	Clothes do not make the man
No pongas todos los huevos en la misma cesta	Do not put all your eggs in the same basket
Las apariencias engañan	Do not judge a book by its cover
La belleza depende del ojo con que se mire	Beauty is in the eye of the beholder
Perro que ladra no muerde	Barking dogs never bite
Las acciones dicen más que las palabras	Actions speak louder than words
De tal palo, tal astilla	Like father, like son
El que mucho abarca, poco aprieta	If you run after two hares, you will catch neither

CHAPTER 25
GRAMMAR SYNTHESIS

Nouns and articles

The nouns in Spanish are separated into two types: masculine and feminine. All nouns, persons and objects are part of one of these groups. Most of the nouns that end with o are masculine and most of the nouns that end with a are feminine.

Masculine	Feminine
Masculino	Jirafa
Cuaderno	Carpeta
Vestido	Crema
Libro	Historia
Zapato	Silla
Escritorio	Botella

Plural nouns

	Add s to nouns that end with a vowel		Add es to nouns that end with a consonant		Nouns that end in z change z by c	
Singular	Perro	Jirafa	Marcador	León	Lápiz	Tapiz
Plural	Perros	Jirafas	Marcadores	Leones	Lápices	Tapices

Articles

These words mark the gender of the nouns.

	Definitive articles		Infinitive articles	
	Feminine	Masculine	Feminine	Masculine
Singular	La	El	Una	Un
	La casa	El elefante	Una pera	Un queso
Plural	Las	Los	Unas	Unos
	Las casas	Los elefantes	Unas peras	Unos quesos

Adjectives

These words describe the nouns. They must agree on gender and number with the noun that modifies.

	Feminine	Masculine
Singular	Manzana roja	Avión grande
Plural	Manzanas rojas	Aviones grandes

Demonstrative articles

They are used the same way as pronouns and must match gender and number with the nouns.

	Near		Not near/ near far			Not far	
	Feminine	Masculine	Feminine	Masculine		Feminine	Masculine
Singular	Esta	Este	Esa	Ese		Aquella	Aquel
	Esta niña	Este oso	Esa ciudad	Ese país		Aquella casa	Aquel árbol
Plural	Esta	Estos	Esas	Esos		Aquellas	Aquellos
	Estas niñas	Estos osos	Esas ciudades	Esos países		Aquellas casas	Aquellos árboles

Possessive adjectives

They show relationship or ownership between people and must match only in number with the noun.

Singular		Plural	
Masculine	Feminine	Masculine	Feminine
Mi perro	Mi gata	Mis perros	Mis gatas
Tu libro	Tu pintura	Tus libros	Tus pinturas
Su pantalón	Su lámpara	Sus pantalones	Sus lámparas
Nuestro barco	Nuestra casa	Nuestros barcos	Nuestras casas

Comparatives

They are used to compare nouns (people or things).

Comparisons of inequality		
Más	Adjective Adverb nouns	Que
Menos		

173

Comparisons of quality		
Tan	Adjective or adverb	Como
Tanto/as	Noun	

Questions

¿Quién?	¿Cómo?	¿Cuándo?	¿Dónde?
¿Por qué?	¿Cuál?	¿Qué?	¿Quiénes?
¿Cuáles?	¿Cuánto?	¿De dónde?	¿Con quién?

Adverbs

- Siempre- always
- Casi siempre- almost always
- Muchas veces/ regularmente- often
- A veces- sometimes
- Casi nunca- almost never
- Nunca- never

Verbs

Present tense of regular verbs

Yo	Camino	Nosotros	Caminamos
Tú	Caminas	Ustedes	Caminan
Ella/él/usted	Camina	Ellos/ellas	Caminan

Present tense of irregular verbs

Ser y estar (to be)

	Ser	Estar
Yo	Soy	Estoy
Tú	Eres	Estás
Ella/él/usted	Es	Está
Nosotros/as	Somos	Estamos
Vosotros/as	Sois	Estáis
Ellos/ellas/ustedes	Son	Están

Ir- to go.

Yo	Voy	Nosotros	Vamos
Tú	Vas	Ustedes	Van
Ella/él/usted	Va	Ellos/ellas	Van

Simple past tense

Yo	Habl**é**	Nosotros	Habl**amos**
Tú	Habl**aste**	Ustedes	Habl**aron**
Ella/él/usted	Habl**ó**	Ellos/ellas	Habl**aron**

Present continuous

Yo	Estoy	Nosotros	Estamos
Tú	Estás	Vosotros	Estáis
Ella/él/usted	Está	Ellos/ustedes	Están

Simple future tense

Persona	Final	Caminar	Beber	Vivir
Yo	É	Caminaré	Beberé	Viviré
Tú	Ás	Caminarás	Beberás	Vivirás
Ella/él/usted	Á	Caminará	Beberá	Vivirá
Nosotros/as	Emos	Caminaremos	Beberemos	Viviremos
Vosotros/as	Éis	Caminaréis	Beberéis	Viviréis
Ellos/ellas/ustedes	Án	Caminarán	Beberán	Vivirán

I am going to

Yo	Voy	Nosotros	Vamos
Tú	Vas	Vosotros	Vais
Ella/él/usted	Va	Ellos/ustedes	Van

CONCLUSION

You have reached the end of your Spanish-learning journey. Don't you feel much more confident in your Spanish now?

You've not only improved your vocabulary significantly, but you have also covered the most commonly used verb conjugations (a complicated subject). You've improved your pronunciation, writing, reading, and speaking.

Your next step is maintenance. Regular practice is key because you don't want to lose what you have already learned. Regular practice doesn't have to be every day, but it should be something that works with your schedule, especially if you have a trip or other occasion to use your Spanish coming up.

Another great idea for improving fluency is to attempt to narrate your day. Make sentences about what you are doing. If you walk into the kitchen, say "Yo voy a la cocina." Then, if you start making a sandwich, say "Yo estoy haciendo un sándwich." If you don't know the word for something, that's a word you need to look up and add to your Spanish notebook.

How can you apply what you have learned?

Look for opportunities to speak. You may have authentic Latino restaurants, corner stores, or hair salons in some areas. Go there instead of your normal place and let them know you want to practice. This is a great way to get some experience with native speakers.

As Spanish speakers would say, "¡Vámonos!"

If you've enjoyed this book, please leave a review so that others eager to learn and explore can benefit from your experience.

EXERCISE ANSWERS

Chapter 2

Connect with lines.

Hello!	¡Buenas noches!
Good morning!	¡Buenos días!
Good afternoon!	¡Hasta pronto!
Good night!	Tengo que irme
See you soon!	¡Adiós!
See you later!	¡Nos vemos!
See you tomorrow!	¡Buenas tardes!
I have to go	¡Hasta mañana!
See you!	¡Hola!
Goodbye!	¡Hasta luego!

Complete the chart.

How are you?	¿Cómo estás? (informal)
How are you?	¿Cómo está usted? (formal)
It is nice to meet you	Mucho gusto
Nice to meet you	Encantado/a
Welcome	Bienvenido/a
I am fine	Estoy bien
I am very tired	Estoy muy cansado/a
I am not OK	No estoy bien
I am sick	Estoy enfermo/a
I am happy	Estoy feliz

How do you say .... in Spanish?

I am from	Soy de …
Where are you from?	Soy de …
My name is	Mi nombre es …
What is your name?	Me llamo …
I live in	Yo vivo en …
Have a good day!	¡Que tengas un buen día!
What is your name?	¿Cómo te llamas?
Where are you from?	¿De dónde eres?

It is time to create yours:

- ¡Buenos **días**!
- ¡Buenos **días**! ¿Cómo **estás**?
- Estoy **muy bien.** ¡**Gracias**! Soy **Mercedes.**
- ¡Bienvenida!
- ¡Encantada! ¿**Cómo estás tú**?
- **Estoy feliz.** ¿**Dónde vives**?
- Vivo en **Miami**
- ¡Que tengas un buen día!
- ¡Adiós!

Finding the correct words.

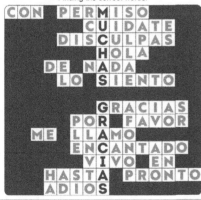

Connect with lines.

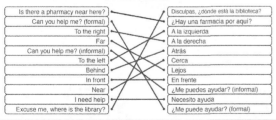

Is there a pharmacy near here?	Disculpas, ¿dónde está la biblioteca?
Can you help me? (formal)	¿Hay una farmacia por aquí?
To the right	A la izquierda
Far	A la derecha
Can you help me? (informal)	Atrás
To the left	Cerca
Behind	Lejos
In front	En frente
Near	¿Me puedes ayudar? (informal)
I need help	Necesito ayuda
Excuse me, where is the library?	¿Me puede ayudar? (formal)

It is time to create yours:

1. Una mandarina es **naranja.**
2. Un plátano es **amarillo.**
3. Un delfín es **gris.**
4. La luna es **blanca.**
5. Un limón es **amarillo.**
6. El cielo es **celeste.**
7. La planta es **verde.**
8. Los colores del semáforo son **rojo, amarillo** y **verde.**

Complete each series:

1. Lunes, **martes**, miércoles, **jueves**, viernes
2. Septiembre, **octubre**, noviembre, **diciembre**, enero
3. Sábado, **domingo, lunes, martes**
4. Marzo, **abril, mayo,** junio, **julio**

Say the numbers in Spanish!

1. Months of the year: **doce (12)**
2. Days of the week: **siete (7)**
3. Hours in a day: **veinticuatro (24)**
4. Sides in one triangle: **tres (3)**
5. Fingers in one hand: **cinco (5)**
6. Fingers in two hands: **diez (10)**
7. Fingers in three hands: **quince (15)**
8. Fingers in ten hands: **cincuenta (50)**
9. Insect legs: **seis (6)**
10. Sides in one square: **cuatro (4)**
11. Sides in two squares: **ocho (8)**
12. Your cell phone number:

Chapter 3

Read these sentences aloud and figure out whom they are talking about based on the list of pronouns above. Connect them with lines

Yo voy a la tienda.	She is my friend.
Ellos estudian todos los días.	We are going to Costa Rica.
Nosotros vamos a Costa Rica.	I am going to the store.
Ella es mi amiga.	They study every day.

Write below what 'the' you think should be used.

Feminine		Masculine	
La	mesa (table)	El	libro (book)
La	silla (chair)	El	disco (disc)
La	planta (plant)	El	equipo (team)
La	manzana (apple)	El	producto (product)
La	pelota (ball)	El	zapato (shoe)
La	muñeca (doll)	El	beso (kiss)
La	vida (life)	El	río (river)
La	respuesta (answer)	El	edificio (building)
La	carta (letter)	El	cuchillo (knife)
La	escuela (school)	El	pueblo (town)

Look at the others on the list and write below what 'the' you think should be used.

Feminine		English word	Masculine	
La	médica	doctor	El	médico
La	empleada	employer	El	empleado
La	gata	cat	El	gato
La	perra	dog	El	perro
La	maestra	teacher	El	maestro
La	jugadora	player	El	jugador
La	arquitecta	architect	El	arquitecto
La	osa	bear	El	oso
La	amiga	friend	El	amigo
La	propietaria	owner	El	propietario

Finally, let's complete some more with little different endings.
If you need to look back on the previous section to identify if a word is masculine or feminine, go ahead and do that.

La	felicidad	La	moto
El	ecosistema	La	actitud
La	amistad	El	programa
La	mano	La	televisión
La	canción	El	síntoma
El	idioma	La	facultad

Identify the correct 'the' needed for each one.

La televisión (the TV)
La contraseña (the password)
Los escritorios (the desks)
El plato (the plate)
Las universidades (the universities)
El cocinero (the cook)
El mapa (the map)
Las motos (the motorbikes)

Subject pronouns
How do you refer to…? ¿Cómo le dirías a…

1. Your best friend? **Tú**
2. Two or more female teachers? **Ellas**
3. Two or more boys? **Ellos**
4. Your mother? **Ella**
5. The President of your country? **Usted**
6. A group of female and male tourists? **Ellos**
7. A group of female soccer players? **Ellas**
8. Yourself? **Yo**
9. Your family? **Nosotros**
10. Your uncle? **Él**

Feminine or masculine?
Recognize each gender and complete the table below using *la* or *el*:

Feminine	Masculine
La mesa	El oso
La planta	El perro
La manzana	El saco
La gata	El huevo
Silla	Baño

Now please, set the same list in the plural forms using *las* or *los*:

Las mesas	Los osos
Las plantas	Los perros
Las manzanas	Los sacos
Las gatas	Los huevos
Las sillas	Los baños

Let's review the use of *el, la, los,* and *las*. Connect with lines

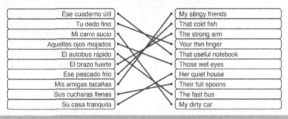

El		mochila
Los		comidas
La		perro
La		tarea
Las		patos

Chapter 4

Set the singular or plural of the following parts:

La espinaca fría	Las espinacas frías
Una lavadora grande	Unas lavadoras grandes
Esa taza caliente	Esas tazas calientes
El tomate pequeño	Los tomates pequeños
Un niño terrible	Unos niños terribles
Mi amigo preocupado	Mis amigos preocupados
El carro limpio	Los carros limpios

Combine articles, nouns, and adjectives.

Ese cuaderno útil	My stingy friends
Tu dedo fino	That cold fish
Mi carro sucio	The strong arm
Aquellos ojos mojados	Your thin finger
El autobus rápido	That useful notebook
El brazo fuerte	Those wet eyes
Ese pescado frío	Her quiet house
Mis amigas tacañas	Their full spoons
Sus cucharas llenas	The fast bus
Su casa tranquila	My dirty car

Let´s do it one more time!

Tus ojos bonitos	Our clean kitchen
Mi plato pequeño	Your beautiful eyes
Esa bicicleta pesada	That bright window
Aquella puerta oscura	My small plate
Nuestra cocina limpia	This polite boy
Esa taza caliente	This hot cup
Este niño educado	That dark door
Aquella ventana luminosa	That closed restaurant
Esta nieve blanda	This heavy bicycle
Aquel restaurante cerrado	This soft snow

Chapter 5

Match the pronouns and the rest of the sentences with lines.

Yo	son niños	Nosotros		es un deportista
Nosotras	es un doctor	Ella		soy ingeniera
Ellos	son muy generosas	Ustedes		es alto
Tú	eres mi amigo	Él		son inteligentes
Ellas	es mi hermano	Yo		eres cocinera
Él	son mexicanos	Ellos		somos hermanos
Usted	somos cantantes	Tú		es de Colombia
Ustedes	soy estudiante	Usted		son amables

Complete the sentences with the missing verb.

Ellos **son** mis hermanos. (They are my brothers.)
Nuestros abuelos son de Madrid, **son** españoles. (Our grandparents are from Madrid, they are Spanish.)
Tú eres muy inteligente. (You're very smart.)
Son las cinco de la tarde. (It's 5 p.m.)
Esta **es** una blusa de seda. (This is a silk blouse.)
Nosotros **somos** muy puntuales. (We are very punctual.)
Estos dos libros **son** de José. (These two books belong to José.)
La fiesta **es** en la casa de Marta. (The party is at Marta's house.)

Let´s find the verbs in the correct form but one step harder.
This time you will have to use all your Spanish knowledge. Get ready!

Pablo **es** de Jamaica y su amigo Joaquín **es** de Colombia. Nosotros **somos** una familia. Yo **soy** de México y mi mamá y mi papá **son** de Ecuador. Mi hermano Raúl **es** de Texas. Él **es** un ingeniero y su mochila **es** azul. Este **es** mi hijo pequeño. Su nombre **es** Diego y su cuaderno **es** grande. Mi teléfono **es** 1-957-11-23-40-00. ¡Adiós! ¡Te veo pronto!

It is time to write complete sentences for the first time.

- Tú eres de Washington y tu gata se llama Frida
- Él es arquitecto y sus productos son muy buenos
- Nosotros somos profesores y José y María son los alumnos.
- Ellos son médicos y su ambulancia es blanca

Complete the following sentences with the correct form of the verb to be.

Ella	está	en Uruguay.
Ellos	están	en la ciudad de San Francisco.
Nosotros	está	en una fiesta.
Él	está	enfermo.
Nosotros	estamos	preocupados.
Yo	estoy	muy feliz.
Ustedes	están	cansados.
Tú	estás	hambriento.
Chile	está	en América del Sur.
Pedro	está	en el juego de fútbol.
Marina y Andrea	están	en el cine.

Rewrite the sentence with the subject pronoun in front.
Look at this example.
Estamos cansados - Nosotros estamos cansados.

Ellos están en la casa.
Tú estás bien.
Usted está en la cama.
Nosotras estamos cerca.
Ella está enojada.
Yo estoy triste.

Estar and *Ser* Practice

Now that you've had the chance to learn both verbs and conjugations, let's do some practice. Translate the following sentences into Spanish.

The girl is happy. **La niña es feliz o la niña está feliz.** (The girl is a happy child or the girl is happy because something special happened to her)
They are friends. **Ellos son amigos or Ellas son amigas.**
We are from the United States. **Nosotros/as somos de los Estados Unidos.**
I am tall. **Yo soy alto/a**
You are tired. **Tú estás cansado/a.**
He is smart. **Él es inteligente.**
It is difficult. **Es difícil.**
The parents are in the house. **Los padres están en la casa.**

Match with lines to make the perfect sentences.

Luis		somos estudiantes de Física
La luna		soy de Mississippi
María y Julieta		están en un partido de fútbol
Mi hermano y yo		es alto y moreno.
El Presidente de los Estados Unidos		está por la noche
Yo		están en la tienda de juguetes
Los niños		es una niña muy atenta
El carro de José		está en su avión
Julia		eres muy gracioso
Yo		estamos solos en la casa
El profesor González		es gris
Tú		estoy muy cansado
Pedro y yo		es en Febrero
Las pelotas de golf		son blancas
El cumpleaños de Tomás		está muy ocupado

Finally, focus on the different uses of *ser* and *estar* and choose one of the two verbs.

- El café **está** muy caliente. The coffee is too hot.
- Mi bicicleta **está** rota. My bike is broken.
- Tu cumpleaños **es** el 3 de enero. Your birthday is on January 3rd.
- Estos zapatos **son** de cuero. These are leather shoes.
- Ella **es** mi mejor amiga. She is my best friend.
- Este carro **es** muy rápido. This car is very fast.
- Nosotros **estamos** de viaje. We are on a trip.
- El desfile **es** en el parque. The parade is in the park.
- Ustedes **son** colombianos. You're Colombians.
- **Estoy** muy resfriado. I have a cold.
- Las verduras **son** muy saludables. Vegetables are very healthy.

Chapter 6

Conjugate the regular verbs escuchar (to listen) and cocinar (to cook)

Yo	escucho	Nosotros	escuchamos
Tú	escuchas	Ustedes	escuchan
Ella/él/usted	escucha	Ellos/ellas	escuchan

Yo	cocino	Nosotros	cocinamos
Tú	cocinas	Ustedes	cocinan
Ella/él/usted	cocina	Ellos/ellas	cocinan

Conjugate the regular verbs aprender (to learn) and correr (to run)

Yo	aprendo	Nosotros	aprendemos
Tú	aprendes	Ustedes	aprenden
Ella/él/usted	aprende	Ellos/ellas	aprenden

Yo	corro	Nosotros	corremos
Tú	corres	Ustedes	corren
Ella/él/usted	corre	Ellos/ellas	corren

Conjugate the regular verbs subir (to go up) and abrir (to open)

Yo	subo	Nosotros	subimos
Tú	subes	Ustedes	suben
Ella/él/usted	sube	Ellos/ellas	suben

Yo	abro	Nosotros	abrimos
Tú	abres	Ustedes	abren
Ella/él/usted	abren	Ellos/ellas	abren

Conjugation Practice

Yo estudio. **I study.**
Ellos compran. **They buy.**
Nosotros vivimos. **We live.**
Tú hablas. **You speak.**
Usted come. **You eat.**
Los niños montan. **The kids ride.**
Yo escribo. **I write.**
Él habla. **He speaks.**
Tú y yo bebemos. **You and I drink.**

Complete the sentences with the correct verbs.

1. Mis amigos y yo **escribimos** cartas a nuestras familias.
2. Manuela y Laura **beben** café en un bar.
3. Yo **corro** por el parque todos los días.
4. Nicolás y Manuel **comen** pizza en un restaurante
5. Tú **vives** en la calle Hudson.
6. Mi abuela **lee** muchos libros.
7. Yo **escucho** canciones de rock.
8. La tienda de comida **abre** a las 11 de la mañana.
9. Yo **bailo** con Pablo.
10. Tú **corres** muy rápido.
11. Él **paga** la entrada de cine.
12. Nosotros **leemos** El Quijote de la Mancha.

Let´s conjugate the verbs in the right way!

1. ¡Pedro es muy inteligente! **habla** inglés, francés, alemán y un poco de mandarín.
2. ¿**Bajan ellos** por la escalera de incendios?
3. ¿Qué **estudias**?
4. ¿**Desayunamos** juntos?
5. Tus padres **escuchan** a todos.
6. ¿Dónde **trabajan ellos**?
7. Mi hermana **vive** muy cerca de la universidad.
8. Tú **comprendes** a tus hijos.
9. Ella **baila** muy bien.
10. Él **cocina** para un restaurante.

Write your own sentences.
Choose the words from each column to create your own sentences.

- María y yo cocinamos pasteles todos los días.
- Los niños pasean por las tiendas los domingos.
- Pedro y Carlos estudian italiano por la noche.
- El amigo de José practica deportes los viernes.
- La señora García toca el piano los lunes.
- Ustedes comen pasta los sábados y domingos.
- Ella mira películas después de la escuela.

Chapter 7

Connect with lines to create sentences.

Mi amigo y yo	juega fútbol en el parque con sus amigos
Nosotras	voy a la casa de mi amigo Pedro
Julieta y Pablo	jugamos ajedrez en la casa de mi abuela
Ella	vamos de compras los fines de semana
Yo	juegan béisbol profesionalmente
Ustedes	van a la biblioteca en el tiempo libre
Los maestros de mi escuela	van a la piscina en verano
Ellos	van a la playa los sábados y domingos

Write three sentences about things you plan to do this week. Remember that you can always look up some new words, but here are a few prompts to get you started.

Yo voy a **pasar un rato con mis amigos**- I am going to hang out with friends
Yo voy a **mirar televisión**- I am going to watch TV
Yo voy a **visitar** a mi amiga Teresa- I am going to visit my friend Teresa.
Yo voy a **manejar** hacia la playa- I am going to drive to the beach.

_____
_____
_____

Irregular Verb Practice

You know what these verbs mean, so let's do a little practice.

Select the verb with the meaning that would make sense with each sentence and conjugate the verb to match the person.

Your options for this first practice are only the irregular verbs- *ir, venir, traer, poner, hacer, tener,* and *decir.*

Mi padre **hace** un pastel (a cake) para mi cumpleaños (birthday).
Mi amiga **tiene** dos mascotas, un perro y un gato.
Yo **pongo** un pastel en el horno (oven).
Ellos **ponen** las mochilas en la mesa.
Yo **digo** "feliz cumpleaños".
Tú **vas** a la tienda.
Yo **voy** a estudiar a la noche (at night).
Yo **traigo** un libro para mi amigo.

Chapter 8

Practice these phrases by completing the conversation with someone you have just met. Write how you would respond to their sentence, then read the conversation aloud.

- Hola, buenos días.
- **¡Buenos días!**
- ¿Cómo está usted?
- **Yo estoy muy bien.**
- Estoy bien, gracias.
- **¿Cómo se llama?**
- Me llamo José. ¿Y usted?
- **Mi nombre es Fernanda.**
- Mucho gusto.
- **Encantada.**

It is time to create another one:

- ¡Buenas **tardes**!
- ¡Buenas **tardes**! ¿Cómo **está** usted?
- Estoy **bien. Gracias** ¿Y usted?
- **Estoy muy bien ¡Gracias**
- **¿Cómo se llama?**
- **Mi nombre es Juan. Tengo 50 años. ¿Y usted?**
- **Me llamo Daniel y tengo 45 años.**
- ¡Que tenga usted un buen día!
- ¡Lo mismo para usted! ¡Adiós!

Hola, me llamo Viviana. Tengo quince años. Vivo en Puerto Rico, pero soy de Colombia. Yo vivo en mi casa con mi madre y mi padre. También tengo cuatro mascotas: dos perros y dos gatos. Voy a la escuela y después, voy a la piscina con mis amigos.

1. ¿Cuántos años tiene Viviana?
Viviana tiene quince años

2. ¿Dónde (where) vive Viviana?
Viviana vive en su casa, con su madre y su padre en Puerto Rico

3. ¿Qué edad tiene Viviana?
Viviana tiene cuatro mascotas.

Chapter 9

¿Cuándo es la independencia de los Estados Unidos?
La independencia de los Estados Unidos es **el 4 de julio.**

¿Cuándo es Noche de Brujas (Halloween)?
La Noche de Brujas es **31 de octubre**

Practice writing sentences to tell what today's date is.

a. 30/5	**Hoy es treinta de mayo.**
b. 18/2	**Hoy es dieciocho de febrero.**
c. 20/7	**Hoy es veinte de julio.**
d. 25/12	**Hoy es veinticinco de diciembre.**
e. 9/6	**Hoy es 9 de junio.**

Read these example sentences and try to figure out what time it is.

a. Son las cinco y media.	**5:30hs.**
b. Son las diez y cuarto.	**10:15hs.**
c. Son las doce menos cinco.	**11:55hs.**
d. Es la una y diez.	**1:10hs.**
e. Son las once y veinte.	**11:20hs.**
f. Son las ocho menos diez.	**7:50hs.**

Let´s practice one more time! Connect with lines

Son las ocho y diez.	7:15 hs
Son las diez menos diez.	8:10hs
Son las tres menos veinte.	4:45 hs
Son las cuatro y veinte.	9:50hs
Son las doce y veinticinco.	2:40 hs
Son las ocho menos veinticinco	12:25 hs
Son las cinco menos cuarto	4:20 hs
Son las siete y cuarto	7:35hs

Practice writing the following times out in full sentences.
Remember to start with *Es la* or *Son las*.

4:30 **Son las cuatro y media.**
10:20 **Son las diez y veinte.**
7:15 **Son las siete y cuarto.**
8:55 **Son las nueve menos cinco.**

Choose the correct time:

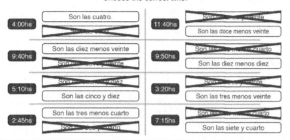

4:00hs	Son las cuatro.	11:40hs	~~Son las doce menos veinte~~
	~~Son las cuatro y veinte~~		Son las doce menos veinte
9:40hs	Son las diez menos veinte	9:50hs	~~Son las diez menos cuarto~~
	~~Son las nueve y veinte~~		Son las diez menos diez
5:10hs	~~Son las cinco y diez~~	3:20hs	~~Son las tres y veinte~~
	Son las cinco y diez		Son las tres menos veinte
2:45hs	Son las tres menos cuarto	7:15hs	~~Son las siete menos cuarto~~
	~~Son las dos y cuarto~~		Son las siete y cuarto

Answer the following questions using the vocabulary and information you have learned in this chapter.

- ¿Qué hora es? **Son las cinco y diez.**
- ¿A qué hora tienes clase de español? **Yo tengo clase de español a las seis de la tarde.**
- ¿A qué hora es la película del cine? **La película del cine es a las siete de la tarde.**
- ¿A qué hora es el programa de TV? **El programa de TV es a las diez de la noche.**
- ¿A qué hora desayunas? **Yo desayuno a las siete de la mañana.**

Write the following times in full sentences.

- 2:30 **Son las dos y media.**
- 12:10 **Son las doce y diez.**
- 4:15 **Son las cuatro y cuarto**
- 10:55 **Son las once menos cinco.**

Putting It All Together

Complete this dialogue.

- ¡Hola! ¡Buenas tardes! **Me llamo** Pedro
- ¡Buenas tardes, Pedro! Soy **Esteban** ¿**Cómo está** usted?
- Estoy **muy bien ¡Gracias! ¿De dónde es usted?**
- Yo soy de **Uruguay** ¿y usted?
- Yo soy de **México**, pero vivo en **Estados Unidos.**
- ¡Un gusto en conocerlo!¡Adiós!
- ¡Hasta pronto!

¿La, el, las o los?

La	casa	El	perro	La	mesa
La	carpeta	Los	cepillos	La	cuchara
El	regalo	La	manzana	Las	tortugas
La	planta	Las	sillas	El	vaso
Los	candados	El	caballo	Las	gatas

Choose an adjective for each noun

tío	grande	perro	cansado	comida	deliciosa
lavadora	vacía	pantalón	roto	pelota	amarilla
camión	lleno	elefante	hambriento	libro	interesante

Choose a noun for each adjective

elefante	pesado	niño	comunicativo	pantalón	sucio
mosquito	liviano	vaso	frío	señor	triste
café	caliente	perro	inquieto	casa	limpia

Complete the tables

Five feminine nouns	Five masculine adjectives
Calle	Serio
Cacerola	Honesto
Cuchara	Trabajador
Taza	Musculoso
Araña	Ventoso

Five Singular Words	Five Plural Words
Piso	Sillones
Techo	Almohadones
Pared	Insectos
Cortina	Ramas
canasto	Flores

Complete the sentences with the proper colors

Los colores de la bandera de los Estados Unidos son **rojo, azul y blanco.**
La lechuga es **verde.**
El chocolate es **marrón.**
Y el café es **negro.**
Me gustan las fresas **moradas.**

Which days or months are missing?

lunes	martes	miércoles	**Jueves**	Viernes
jueves	viernes	sábado	Domingo	**lunes**
agosto	septiembre	**octubre**	noviembre	Diciembre
sábado	**domingo**	lunes	martes	miércoles
junio	julio	agosto	septiembre	Octubre
diciembre	enero	**febrero**	marzo	abril

Complete the sentences using the correct verbs.

Yo **tengo** diez años.
Los padres **viven** en los Estados Unidos.
Nosotros **caminamos** por la playa todos los días.
Mi cumpleaños **es** el miércoles 8 de febrero.
María **cocina** un rico pastel de chocolate.
Usted siempre **come** verduras.
Ellos **están** en reunión de trabajo ahora.
Mi hermano **vende** su bicicleta azul.
Mariano **escribe** para un periódico de noticias.
María y José **compramos** pan y hamburguesas.

Change the verb to match the person.

Yo **enseño**
Nosotros **comemos**
Él **bebe**
Tú **manejo**
Mis amigos **van**
Yo **voy**
Usted **pone**
Yo **tengo**

Chapter 10

Find a question for each answer.

Tú duermes.	¿Tú duermes?
Él cocina.	¿Él cocina?
Nosotros vamos a la playa.	¿Nosotros vamos a la playa?
Ella escribe.	¿Ella escribe?
Tú hablas.	¿Tú hablas?
Ellos pasean.	¿Ellos pasean?
Usted come.	¿Usted come?
Ustedes cenan acá.	¿Ustedes cenan aca?

Connect with lines.

¿Compras un poco de queso?	No, nosotros no bailamos tango.
¿Lees las noticias todos los días?	No, no limpio mi dormitorio.
¿Quieres beber un jugo de naranja?	No, no quiero beber un jugo de naranja.
¿Bailan tango ustedes?	No, no juego mucho al golf.
¿Limpias tu dormitorio?	No, no compro un poco de queso.
¿Juegas mucho al golf?	No, mis manos no están sucias.
¿Es un día soleado?	No, no leo las noticias todos los días
¿Están sucias tus manos?	No, no es un día soleado.

Answer these questions by yourself using a negative form as an example.

¿Traen ustedes un regalo?	No, nosotros no traemos un regalo.
¿Cantan ustedes una canción?	No, nosotrosno cantamos una canción.
¿Juega tenis?	No, él no juega tenis.
¿Comes pastel de manzanas?	No, yo no como pastel de manzanas.
¿Compras un pantalón azul?	No, yo no compro un pantalón azul.
¿Practica ejercicio todos los días?	No, ella no practica ejercicio todos los días.
¿Tenemos comida suficiente para todos?	No, no tenemos comida suficiente para todos.
¿Estudias en la mañana o en la noche?	No, yo no estudio ni a la mañana ni a la noche.
¿Comes mucha pizza?	No, yo no como mucha pizza.
¿Manejas un carro?	No, yo no manejo un carro.
¿Estudias para el examen?	No, yo no estudio para el examen.
¿Ordenamos un poco esta casa?	No, no ordenamos un poco esta casa.

Now answer the following questions by yourself.

- ¿Cómo se llama la película?
- **La película se llama Chicago.**

- ¿Dónde están tus zapatos?
- **Mis zapatos están en el carro.**

- ¿Cuál es el número de teléfono de aquí?
- **El número de teléfono es xxx-xxx-xxxx.**

- ¿Quién es Tomás?
- **Tomás es mi hermano.**

- ¿Qué día es tu cumpleaños?
- **Mi cumpleaños es el 15 de noviembre.**

- ¿Cuántas pizzas ordeno?
- **Ordena 5 pizzas para todos.**

- ¿Qué traes en tu mochila?
- **Traigo en mi mochila 2 libros, 3 cuadernos y unos lápices de colores.**

- ¿Cuántos libros tienes en la mesa?
- **En la mesa tengo 10 libros.**

Answer these questions by yourself using a negative form as an example.

Where are you going to?	Yo voy a la playa.
Which school do you go to?	Yo voy a la Escuela Madison.
Whom are you going with?	Yo voy con mi amiga Betty.
Whom are you cooking with?	Yo cocino con mi mamá.
Who is this shirt for?	Esta camiseta es para mi hijo.
What is this book about?	Este libro es de Geografía.

Create sentences to give the following information.

- There is a bed in the bedroom. **Hay una cama en mi dormitorio.**

- There are children at the park. **Hay niños en el parque.**

- There is a lot of fruit. **Hay mucha fruta.**

- There is water on the table. **Hay agua sobre la mesa.**

Chapter 11

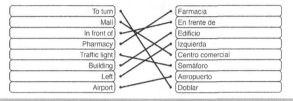

To turn	Farmacia
Mall	En frente de
In front of	Edificio
Pharmacy	Izquierda
Traffic light	Centro comercial
Building	Semáforo
Left	Aeropuerto
Airport	Doblar

Try to answer these questions in Spanish using the previous verbs and the vocabulary from this lesson.

¿Cómo puedo llegar al aeropuerto?
- Toma el bus 86. La parada está frente a esa farmacia.

¿Adónde tienes que ir?
- Tengo que ir al Museo de Arte.

¿Dónde hay una farmacia?
- Camina derecho cinco cuadras y dobla a la izquierda. La farmacia está a tu izquierda.

Estoy perdido. ¿Sabes dónde está la catedral?
- Sí. Camina derecho cinco cuadras por aquí, dobla a tu derecha y camina otras tres cuadras. Ahí está la Catedral.

¿Cuántas cuadras debo caminar para llegar al Museo de Arte Moderno?
- Camina quince cuadras por la calle Adams.

Necesito ir a la estación de trenes. ¿Puedo caminar desde aquí?
- Sí, camina derecho por aquí por 11 cuadras. La estación de tren está al final de esta calle.

Chapter 12

Connect with lines to create the correct sentences.

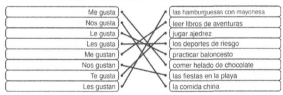

Me gusta	las hamburguesas con mayonesa
Nos gusta	leer libros de aventuras
Le gusta	jugar ajedrez
Les gusta	los deportes de riesgo
Me gustan	practicar baloncesto
Nos gustan	comer helado de chocolate
Te gusta	las fiestas en la playa
Les gustan	la comida china

Now, it is time to write your own sentences:

Me gusta **caminar sin zapatos por la playa.**
Les gusta **mirar la luna llena sobre las montañas.**
Te gustan **los paseos a caballo.**

Let´s continue with your own sentences.

A mi mamá le gusta **visitar a sus amigas y tomar te con ellas.**
A mí me gusta **ir al teatro y al cine.**
A tus hijos les gusta **jugar a las escondidas en la casa de la abuela.**
A esas mujeres les gusta **hacer compras en el Paseo de la Plaza.**

If you want to talk about dislikes, then you should place *no* before the pronoun:

No me gusta esta canción.	I don't like this song.
No me gusta el café frío.	I do not like cold coffee.
No me gustan los días lluviosos.	I do not like rainy days.

Answer the following questions.

¿Te gustan las películas de terror? Do you like horror films?
No, no me gustan las películas de terror.

¿Te gusta el café con azúcar? Do you like coffee with sugar?
No, no me gusta el café con azúcar.

¿Te gustan los museos de arte moderno? Do you like modern art museums?
No, no me gustan los museos de arte moderno.

¿Te gusta el calor o el frío? Do you like hot or cold weather?
No, no me gusta el frío. Me gusta el calor.

¿Te gusta el mar o te gustan las montañas? Do you like the sea or the mountains?
No me gusta el mar, ni me gustan las montañas. Me gusta el campo.

¿Te gusta o no te gusta? Complete these sentences.

Me gusta montar a caballo.
No me gusta tocar la guitarra.
Me gusta beber leche caliente.
Me gusta leer un libro de amor.
No me gusta comer arroz con chocolate.
Me gusta trabajar en un parque de diversiones.
No me gusta tocar arañas con las manos.

Based on the following people´s personalities, write two sentences expressing likes and dislikes. You can follow the example below.

Eres una persona deportista. (libros/entrenamientos)
  • No te gusta leer libros.
  • Te gusta hacer entrenamientos al aire libre.

Mis hermanos Tomás y Martín son atléticos. (bailar/practicar deportes)
  • No les gusta bailar.
  • Les gusta practicar deportes.

Soy muy romántica. (películas de amor/películas de guerras)
  • Me gustan las películas de amor.
  • No me gustan las películas de guerras.

Teresa tiene muchos amigos. (fiestas/caminar sola)
  • Le gustan las fiestas.
  • No le gusta caminar sola.

Express your opinion about these topics using the previous verbs. (Example exercises)

No me gusta la gente soberbia.	- Arrogant people
No me gustan las películas de acción.	- Action movies
No me gusta el tráfico.	- Traffic
No me gusta el humo del cigarrillo.	- Cigarette smoke
Me gusta la historia estadounidense.	- American History
Me gustan los viajes al extranjero.	- Traveling abroad
No me gustan las mentiras.	- Lies
Me gusta la comida asiática.	- Asian food

Now, tell somebody else's opinion about the previous topics.
Remember to change the pronoun! For example, *A mi hermano le encanta las películas de acción. (Example answers)*

A mi papá no le gusta la gente soberbia.	- Arrogant people
A mi hija le encantan las películas de acción.	- Action movies
A mi hermano le fastidia el tráfico.	- Traffic
A Juan le molesta el humo del cigarrillo.	- Cigarette smoke
A Martin le encanta la historia estadounidense.	- American History
A mi hermana le interesan los viajes al extranjero.	- Traveling abroad
A Mariano le fastidian las mentiras.	- Lies
A mis amigos les gusta la comida asiática.	- Asian food

Write a sentence using the following elements.

yo / encantar / estudiar español
- Me encanta estudiar español.

él / molestar / viajar en metro
- A él le moslesta viajar en metro.

nosotros / gustar / caminar por la ciudad
- A nosotras nos gusta caminar por la ciudad.

ellos / aburrir / escuchar al profesor
- A ellos no les aburre escuchar al profesor.

ustedes / entusiasmar / conocer un nuevo país
- A ustedes les estusiasma conocer un nuevo país.

yo / interesar / leer ficción
- A mi no me interesa leer libros de ficción.

Let´s practice with the verb trabajar (to work)

Yo	trabajé	Nosotros	trabajamos
Tú	trabajaste	Ustedes	trabajaron
Ella/él/usted	trabajó	Ellos/ellas	trabajaron

Practice conjugating these verbs in the PAST tense.
Look up the chart if you need to review the endings.

- Yo/ escuchar **Yo escuché**
- Ellos/ trabajar **Ellos trabajaron**
- Tú y yo/ esperar **Tú y yo esperamos**
- Yo/ buscar **Yo busqué**
- Mi amiga/ llamar **Mi amiga llamó**
- Tú/ manejar **Tú manejaste**
- Yo/ comenzar **Yo comencé**

Let´s practice with the verb correr (to run)

Yo	corrí	Nosotros	corrimos
Tú	corriste	Ustedes	corrieron
Ella/él/usted	corrió	Ellos/ellas	corrieron

Let´s practice with the verb compartir (to share)

Yo	compartí	Nosotros	compartimos
Tú	compartiste	Ustedes	compartieron
Ella/él/usted	compartió	Ellos/ellas	compartieron

Turn these present-tense sentences into past tense.

- Yo dejo mis llaves en la mesa.
  Yo dejé mis llaves en la mesa.

- Ellos no comen nada.
  Ellos no comieron nada.

- Nosotros llamamos a nuestra madre.
  Nosotros llamamos a nuestra madre.

- Tú esperas mucho tiempo.
  Tú esperaste mucho tiempo.

- Yo camino mucho.
  Yo caminé mucho.

- El trabaja poco.
  Él trabajó mucho.

- Los niños saltan en el parque.
  Los niños saltaron en el parque.

- Mis vecinos miran una película en el cine.
  Mis vecinos miraron una película en el cine.

- Rita y Josefina pasean en el centro comercial.
  Rita y Josefina pasearon en el centro comercial.

- La cocinera prepara unos pasteles exquisitos.
  La cocinera preparó unos pasteles exquisitos.

Practice
Answering Questions in Past Tense

Now that you can put on past tense endings instead of the present, let's practice answering some questions using the past tense.

¿A qué hora cenaste anoche? (What time did you have dinner last night?)
Anoche cené a las ocho de la noche.

¿Cuándo estudiaste español? (When did you study Spanish?)
Estudié español en la escuela primaria.

¿A quién llamaste ayer? (Who did you call yesterday?)
Ayer llamé a mi abuela.

¿Qué comiste de almuerzo? (What did you eat for lunch?)
Comí una ensalada de atún.

¿Cuándo llegaron tus amigos? (When did your friends arrive?)
Mis amigos llegaron ayer a la noche.

Let´s practice. For this next exercise, you must first recognize and change the verb tense, moving these sentences into present or past tense.

Ellos estudiaron mucho. **Ellos estudian mucho**

Manejé por cinco horas. **Yo manejo por cinco horas.**

Yo no escribí mucho. **Yo no escribo mucho.**

Nosotros trabajamos en el campo. **Nosotros trabajamos en el campo.**

Tú recibiste cien dólares por tu trabajo. **Tú recibes cien dólares por tu trabajo.**

Él llevó fruta al picnic. **Ella lleva frutas al picnic.**

Ella tomó el bus en frente de la tienda. **Ella toma el bus en frente de la tienda.**

Chapter 14

(Example answer)

Me llamo **María José** y tengo **25 años**. Mi cumpleaños es el **10 de marzo**. Vivo en **Buenos Aites**. Me gusta **jugar tenis, cocinar y leer libros** pero no me gusta **comer vegetales crudos**. Mi actividad favorita es **pasear con mis perros por el campo** y mis colores preferidos son **verde, azul y amarillo**.

What time is it?

Complete the table writing the time with numbers or letters.

Son las doce.	12:00
Son las tres menos diez	2:50
Son las cinco y media.	5:30
Son las ocho y diez	8:10
Es la una.	1:00
Son las tres y veinticinco	3:25
Son las diez y cuarto.	10:15
Son las cuatro y media	4:30
Son las ocho y cuarenta.	8:40
Son las dice menos veinte	11:40

What day is today?

Complete the table writing the time with numbers or letters.

Hoy es lunes 3 de noviembre	3/11
Hoy es jueves 5 de octubre	5/10
La fecha es martes 25 de septiembre	25/9
Hoy es martes 16 de agosto	16/8
Hoy es sábado 7 de diciembre	7/12
Hoy es viernes 1 de noviembre	1/1
La fecha es jueves 15 de febrero	15/2
Hoy es domingo 4 de mayo	4/5
Hoy es domingo 19 de agosto	19/8
Hoy es lunes 7 de junio	7/6

Pronouns, nouns, and adjectives
Connect with lines

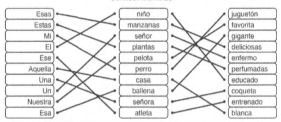

Esas	niño	juguetón
Estas	manzanas	favorita
Mi	señor	gigante
El	plantas	deliciosas
Ese	pelota	enfermo
Aquella	perro	perfumadas
Una	casa	educado
Un	ballena	coqueta
Nuestra	señora	entrenado
Esa	atleta	blanca

Singular, plural, masculine or feminine
Mark with an X in the correct columns

Palabra	singular	plural	femenino	masculino
toalla	X		X	
chocolates		X		X
manzanas		X	X	
silla	X		X	
perros		X		X
cocodrilo	X			X
frutas		X	X	
máquina	X		X	
teléfonos		X		X
botellas		X	X	

Subjects, verbs, and pronouns

Identify the verb and the subject of each pair of sentences and write the correct pronoun in the second one.

- Javier es mi mejor amigo. **Él** es de Madrid, España.
- María y Julieta juegan tenis. **Ellas** no son jugadoras profesionales.
- Francisco tiene un regalo muy especial. **Él** está muy feliz.
- Alicia y Laura son de Costa Rica. **Ellas** bailan salsa todos los días.
- Ricardo es profesor de Química. **Él** trabaja siempre en el laboratorio.
- Juan y Patricio son compañeros de clase. **Ellos** son de México.

Choose the best answer for each question

¿Cuántos años tienes?	Es el 16 de septiembre.
¿Cómo es ese niño?	Yo quiero comer pizza y helado.
¿Quién es tu mejor amigo?	Tengo cuarenta y dos años.
¿Te gustó la película?	Sí. Le encantó. Dijo que estaba delicioso.
¿Cuándo es la Independencia de México?	Es muy tranquilo y alegre.
¿Le gustó el pastel a Rodrigo?	Llega a las 3:40 PM.
¿Quién quiere comer pizza?	Se llama Nicolás González. Es de Perú.
¿Cuándo viene el tren?	No me gustó. Era muy aburrida.

Answer Some Questions

Practice answering these question words.
You may look back at the previous chapters if you have any questions.

- ¿Cómo te llamas?
Me llamo Robin

- ¿Cuántos años tienes?
Tengo veinticuatro años

- ¿Tienes mascotas?
Si, tengo un perro, dos gatos y un conejo.

- ¿Necesitas estudiar?
Sí, necesito estudiar mucho.

- ¿Te gusta el español?
Sí, me encanta el idioma

- ¿Qué hora es?
Son las tres menos cuarto.

- ¿Cuándo es tu cumpleaños?
Mi cumpleaños el es 31 de enero.

- ¿Dónde está tu casa?
Mi casa está en la Avenida Marques. Caminas tres cuadras derecho por aquí y luego doblas a la izquierda y caminas una cuadra más.

- ¿Adónde fuiste ayer?
Ayer fui al teatro con Esteban y Margarita.

- ¿Qué hiciste el domingo?
El domingo salí a correr por el parque. Hice dos vueltas alrededor del lago.

- ¿Cómo eres tú?
Yo soy estudiosa y muy serena. No me gustan los ruidos fuertes y las reuniones con mucha gente.

- ¿Cómo se llama tu mejor amigo? ¿Qué le gusta hacer?
Mi mejor amigo se llama Peter. Él es muy deportista. Le gusta jugar tenis, fútbol montar caballos.

Using the verbs in the correct tense
Complete the paragraph

Yo (ser) **soy** Mario y (jugar) **juego** al fútbol todos los domingos. Me gusta jugar cuando (hacer) **hace** frío y poco calor. Mi mejor amigo se (llamar) **llama** Pedro. Él (practicar) **practica** natación. Así que cuando yo (terminar) **termino** de jugar fútbol, (ir) **voy** a la piscina y los dos juntos (nadar) **nadamos** un rato. Los sábados (ir) **vamos** al centro comercial y (almorzar) **almorzamos** ahi hamburguesas. Cuando nosotros (regresar) **regresamos**, (invitar) **invitamos** a nuestros amigos a mi casa. Pedro (tocar) **toca** la guitarra y yo (cantar) **canto**. Nuestros amigos (bailar) **bailan** y todos nos (reir) **reímos** mucho. Por las noches todos juntos (ir) **vamos** a fiestas y nos (divertir) **divertimos** mucho. Los domingos (descansar) **descansamos**. Me gusta (tener) **tener** amigos como ellos.

Talking about your town
Answer these questions about your city.

- ¿Hay museos en tu ciudad?
Sí, hay muchos museos en mi ciudad.

- ¿Hay una clase de español?
Sí, hay dos clases de español.

- ¿Qué te gusta visitar en tu ciudad?
Me gusta visitar el Parque de la Independencia y el Museo Sívori.

- ¿Qué está en frente de tu casa?
En frente de mi casa está el Paseo de los Niños.

- ¿Hay muchas personas en tu ciudad?
Sí, en mi ciudad hay muchas personas.

Answer these questions about yourself.

- ¿Qué te gusta desayunar?
Me gusta desayunar huevos, yogur y fruta.

- ¿A qué hora te gusta estudiar?
Me gusta estudiar por la mañana.

- ¿Qué tipo de música te gusta escuchar?
Me gusta escuchar rock romántico.

- ¿Te molesta el frío?
No, me encanta el frío

- ¿Con quién te gusta viajar?
Me gusta viajar con mis amigos. Me divierto mucho con ellos.

Complete the missing word.

1. A nosotros **nos** gusta tu apartamento.
2. Me **gusta** ir de vacaciones contigo.
3. A mi mamá **le** encanta la comida italiana.
4. ¿Te **gustan** los libros de cocina?
5. A mí **me** fastidia tanto tráfico.

Past Tense Review

In this exercise, you will practice what you learned in chapter thirteen. As you read the sentences and comprehend the meaning of each one, find the verb in the past.

6. Tú **vendiste** (vender) tu casa vieja.
7. Mis hermanos y yo **fuimos** (ir) a la escuela el viernes.
8. Mi padre **comió** (comer) toda la comida.
9. Yo **estudié** (estudiar) después de la escuela.
10. Lucía **bebió** (beber) jugo.
11. Juan y Julio **fueron** (ir) a ver una película.
12. Hoy, yo **hice** (hacer) mi tarea temprano.
13. Los estudiantes **pusieron** (poner) su tarea en el escritorio.
14. Eduardo **tuvo** (tener) una mascota antes.
15. Tú **olvidaste** (olvidar) estudiar para el examen.

Chapter 15

Family Vocabulary Practice
Based on the tree, who is who?

1. ¿Quién es la hermana de Fernanda?
La hermana de Fernanda es Estela.

2. ¿Quiénes son las hermanas de Carlos?
Las hermanas de Carlos son Paola, María y Susana.

3. ¿Quién es el esposo de Nora?
El esposo de Nora es Eduardo

4. ¿Quién es el papá de Alberto?
El papá de Alberto es Diego.

5. ¿Quién es la tía de Carlos?
La tía de Carlos es Fernanda.

6. ¿Quién es el abuelo de Pedro?
El abuelo de Pedro es Eduardo.

7. ¿Quién es el cuñado de Diego?
El cuñado de Diego es Rodolfo.

8. ¿Quién es la cuñada de Rodolfo?
La cuñada de Rodolfo es Fernanda.

9. ¿Quiénes son los primos de Inés?
Los primos de Inés son Paola, Carlos, María y Susana.

10. ¿Quiénes son las primas de Paola?
Las primas de Paola son Inés y Andrea.

Actividades en familia

Complete using the correct conjugation of the present tense and read aloud.

Las familias latinas (ser) **son** muy unidas y les (gustar) **gusta** (hacer) **hacer** muchas actividades juntos. (Pasear) **Pasean** todos juntos, (celebrar) **celebran** cumpleaños y se (visitar) **visitan** con frecuencia. (ser) **Son** familias que se (acompañar) **acompañan** y se (ayudar) **ayudan** y a menudo (vivir) **viven** cerca.

Solve the following riddles and guess which family member is being described.

1. Es el hermano de tu mamá. **Mi tío**
2. Es el papá de tu papá. **Tu abuelo**
3. Es la hija de tu mamá. **Mi hermana**
4. Es el hijo de tu hermano. **Mi sobrino**
5. Es el hermano de tu esposo. **Mi cuñado**

Complete this dialogue between two brothers using the verbs in the box.

CREO - FUE – TUVE – ESTUVO – JUGUEMOS - TENGO - NECESITO – PREPARÓ – ESTÁ – QUIERES – VISITAR- ESTUDIAR- ESTÁ – REGRESA - FUE

Juan: ¡Hola José! ¿Cómo te **FUE** en la escuela?
José: **CREO** que bien. **TUVE** un examen de Química y **NECESITO** estudiar para mi prueba de Biología que será mañana. ¿Y tú?
Juan: Mi día **ESTUVO** muy bueno pero **TENGO** mucha hambre.
José: Mamá **PREPARÓ** un pastel de coco. **ESTÁ** delicioso.
Juan: ¡Que rico! ¡Gracias! ¿**QUIERES** jugar un rato afuera en el parque?
José: **JUGUEMOS** un rato porque tengo que **ESTUDIAR**.
Juan: ¿Sabes dónde **ESTÁ** mamá?
José: Sí, ella se **FUE** a **VISITAR** a la tía Elena.

Answer these questions about your family.

1. ¿Cuántos hermanos tienes?
- **Tengo cinco hermanos**

2. ¿Tu familia es grande o pequeña?
- **Mi familia es grande.**

3. ¿Cómo es tu tío?
- **Mi tío es el hermano mayor de mi mamá. Es muy bueno y cocina muy bien.**

4. ¿Tienes sobrinos?
- **Sí, tengo diez sobrinos.**

Family Vocabulary Reading

1. ¿Cuántos años tienen los hermanos de Marta?
- **Los hermanos de Marta tienen veinticuatro y veintidós años.**

2. ¿Cuántos primos tiene?
- **Marta tiene cuatro primos.**

3. ¿A qué le gusta jugar a Valeria?
- **A Valeria le gusta jugar a las escondidas.**

4. ¿Dónde busca Marta?
- **Marta busca a Valeria en la casa.**

5. ¿Quién ayuda a Marta?
- **El tío ayuda a Marta.**

Chapter 16

(Example answers)

¿Dónde vives?
Yo vivo en un apartamento pequeño con vista al mar.

¿Cuál es tu lugar favorito para vivir?
Mi lugar favorito para vivir está en las montañas

¿Te gustan las casas rodantes o las casas de campo?
Me gustan las casas rodantes y las casas de campo.

¿Prefieres vivir en una casa o un apartamento?
Prefiero vivir en una casa

Complete the sentences with the right place.

- Los platos están en **la cocina.**
- La ducha está en **el baño.**
- Las sábanas están en **los dormitorios**
- El microondas está en **la cocina.**
- El sillón está en **la sala.**
- La cama está en **en dormitorio.**
- Los juguetes están en **el jardín.**
- Los carros están en **el garage.**
- Los cuchillos están **la cocina**
- La toalla está en **el baño.**
- Los osos de peluche están en **el dormitorio.**

Tres objetos que encontramos en (examples)

La cocina	La sala	El dormitorio
Una tostadora	Unas revistas	Una cama
Una heladera	Un sillón	Unas perchas
Un basurero	Una lámpara	Un colchón

Tres objetos que NO encontramos en

El baño	El parque	El garaje
Un lavaplatos	Un ascensor	Un escritorio
Un microondas	Una cafetera	Una mesa de luz
Las ollas	Una bañadera	Las sábanas

Tres objetos de la casa que empiezan con la letra

A	M	S
La almohada	El mantel	La sartén
La aspiradora	La mesa	La silla
Las alacenas	El microondas	El sillón

Tres objetos de la casa que terminan con la letra

R	O	N
El televisor	El vaso	El tazón
El repasador	El horno	El jabón
El tenedor	El florero	El edredón

Is it V (VERDADERO) (TRUE) or F (FALSO) (FALSE). Mark the correct V or F

V	F	
	X	Hay una cama y un papel higiénico en el jardín de mi casa.
X		Hay una almohada y un colchón en el dormitorio de mi casa.
	X	Hay un sillón en la cocina de mi casa.
	X	Hay un microondas en el baño de mi casa.
	X	Hay un refrigerador en mi dormitorio.
X		Hay una mesa y una silla en la cocina de mi casa.
	X	Hay una cafetera y un cuchillo en el jardín de mi casa

Adjectives that describe your home. Circle those that apply. Mi casa es

luminosa | grande | linda | fría

pequeña | moderna | Vieja | fea

desordenada | cálida | Ordenada | cómoda

Mi casa es **grande, luminosa, cálida y**

Adjectives that describe your bedroom. Circle those that apply.
(example) Mi dormitorio es

luminoso | grande | lindo | frío

pequeño | moderno | Viejo | feo

desordenado | cálido | Ordenado | cómodo

Mi dormitorio es **cómodo, moderno y muy**

Home activities. Who does what?
Complete the chart with the person who does this task at your house.

Cortar el césped	Mi papá	Hacer las compras	Mi papá
Pasar la aspiradora	Mi mamá	Sacar la basura	Mi papá
Limpiar el baño	Mi hermano	Ordenar	Todos
Lavar los platos	Mi hermana	Barrer	Mi hermana
Cocinar	Yo	Hacer las camas	Mi mamá
Limpiar la cocina	Mi hermano	Arreglar la sala	Mi mamá

Now write the sentences indicating who in your family does each task.
For example. Mi papa corta el césped.

- Mi papá corta el césped en el fin de semana.
- Mi mamá pasa la aspiradora por las alfombras.
- Mi hermano limpia el baño.
- Mi hermana lava los platos por las noches.
- Yo cocino una vez por semana.
- Mi hermano limpia la cocina.
- Mi papá hace las compras en el supermercado.
- Mi papá saca la basura todos los días.
- Todos ordenamos en casa.
- Mi hermana barre el piso del comedor y su dormitorio.
- Mi mamá hace las camas todas las mañanas.
- Mi mamá siempre arregla la sala.

Find the preposition in each sentence.

- Yo voy a la biblioteca **para** leer **en** silencio.
- Yo camino alrededor **de** la cancha **de** béisbol cuando no llueve.
- Yo estoy **con** mis amigos **desde** las diez de la mañana.
- Yo juego **contra** ellos **bajo** presión.
- Yo soy **de** los Estados Unidos.
- El título **del** libro es interesante, pero **entre** nosotros, es muy aburrido.
- Llueve **desde** ayer de la noche.
- El lápiz está **bajo** la silla.
- El cuaderno azul está **en** la mochila **de** mi amigo.
- Ellos están **en** clase **de** Biología.
- Yo no puedo escoger **entre** la manzana y la naranja.
- El gato está **sobre** el sofá.
- Mis vecinos están **sin** mi ayuda para preparar el festival.
- El juguete está **entre** la caja y la silla.
- Yo trabajo **hasta** las cinco de **la** tarde.
- La comida es **para** mí porque estoy **sin** almorzar.
- Me gusta el café **sin** azúcar.
- El cielo gris está **sobre** las montañas.
- El avión vuela **hacia** Miami **con** escala **en** Panamá.
- Elizabeth está **en contra de** tu opinión.
- Según los médicos, su estado **de** salud es estable, pero sigue delicado.
- La masa se trabaja **mediante** golpes suaves.
- Lo de siempre: Oriente **versus** Occidente.
- Hubo muchos gritos y golpes **durante** el partido de fútbol.

Read the sentences below and figure out
which preposition would be appropriate to complete the sentence.

- Yo camino de mi casa **hacia** mi trabajo. (hint- if you're going from one place, it would only make sense that you are going to another place)
- Ellos toman su café **sin** azúcar. (hint- they don't like sugar)
- El perro está **en** su casa. (hint- the dog doesn't like the cold outside)
- El techo (ceiling or roof) está **sobre** las camas. (hint- where would it make sense for the roof to be in relation to the beds?)
- La farmacia está **entre** las dos tiendas. (hint- there is a store on either side of the pharmacy)

Reading Comprehension

¿Cuántos dormitorios hay en la casa nueva?
La casa nueva tiene cuatro dormitorios.

¿Hay un sótano o un ático en la casa?
La casa nueva tiene un sótano.

¿Qué quiso comprar la madre?
La madre de Marcos quiso comprar dos camas y un sofá.

¿Cuándo se mudan?
Ellos se mudan el quince de febrero.

House Practice

Read the following sentences and take them as an example.

Mi casa tiene dos baños. Un baño está cerca de la cocina y el otro baño está cerca de mi dormitorio. En mi dormitorio hay dos lámparas y una cama. La cama es grande y rosada. No tengo alfombra en mi dormitorio. Hay otro dormitorio, pero lo uso como oficina. Tengo un escritorio y una silla. También, mi computadora está allí. Hay una televisión en mi sala, pero no hay televisión en mi dormitorio.

Write a description of where you live. Add as many details as you like.

Yo vivo en una casa grande y blanca. Mi casa se construyó en 1998. Tiene 4 dormitorios, 4 baños, una sala muy grande, un comedor, un escritorio y una cocina amplia. Además, tiene un sector de lavandería y un hermoso jardín con flores, una huerta y una piscina. Mi casa no tiene sótano, pero tiene un ático donde guardamos muchas cosas. Es una casa cómoda para nosotros. Podemos recibir visitas y hacer fiestas con muchas personas.

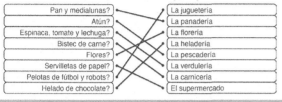

Chapter 17

Connect with lines. Where do you buy...

Pan y medialunas?	La juguetería
Atún?	La panadería
Espinaca, tomate y lechuga?	La florería
Bistec de carne?	La heladería
Flores?	La pescadería
Servilletas de papel?	La verdulería
Pelotas de fútbol y robots?	La carnicería
Helado de chocolate?	El supermercado

Now, it is time to create una "lista de supermercado".

Imagine that you want to bake a birthday cake. You will need eggs, butter, sugar, flour, vanilla, chocolate, cream, and candles. Can you make a list with quantities in Spanish?

- ✅ 12 huevos
- ✅ 1 pan de manteca
- ✅ 1 paquete de azúcar
- ✅ 1 paquete de harina
- ✅ 1 extracto de vainilla
- ✅ 2 potes de chocolate
- ✅ 3 potes de crema
- ✅ 2 paquetes de velas

Now, imagine that you want to invite your friends to a pizza night at your house. Make your Spanish list including drinks, appetizers, napkins, and desserts.

- **Platos descartables**	- **Vasos descartables**
- **Servilletas**	- **Papas chips**
- **Queso**	- **Tomate**
- **Lechuga**	- **Hamburguesas**
- **Pan de hamburguesas**	- **Soda**
- **Agua**	- **Helados**
- **Jugos**	- **Aderezos**
- **Mostaza**	- **Copetín**
- **Mayonesa**	- **Cebolla**
- **Café**	- **Té**
- **Frutas como manzanas, uvas, plátanos**	

Now, write your own story. (Example story)

Hoy es un día lluvioso. Es un feo día para salir de compras, pero voy al supermercado con mi mamá porque en mi casa tenemos pocos alimentos. Mamá busca un carro y yo busco otro. Así compramos más rápido. Tenemos dos listas diferentes. Mamá busca aceite, vinagre, arroz, fideos, tomates azúcar y cereales. Yo busco huevos, yogur, leche, quesos, carne, verduras, frutas y productos de limpieza. Cuando terminamos, nos juntamos en la fila del cajero y esperamos a que nos atiendan. Pasamos todos los productos y una señora muy amable nos ayuda a guardar todo en bolsas de papel. Mi mamá usa su tarjeta de crédito para pagar. Compramos mucho, pero creo que estaremos muchos días sin volver al supermercado.

Find the Spanish words for:

Client	Discount	Cashier	Cash	Label
Brand	Sizes	Offer	Coins	Credit
Fitting room	Cheap	Expensive	Shelf	Basket

Cliente	Descuento	Cajero	Efectivo	etiqueta
Marca	Talles	Oferta	Monedas	Crédito
Probador	Barato	Caro	Estante	Canasto

Connect to create sentences.

Compro manzanas	para preparar el desayuno de los niños.
Necesitas comprar huevos y leche	son deliciosos para preparar un pastel.
María y José	en el supermercado.
María usa su tarjeta de crédito	caminan por el Centro Comercial.
Esos limones	o prefieren pasta para la cena?
¿Les gusta el atún	para pagar las compras en la panadería.

Write the complete sentences below:

1. Compro manzanas **en el supermercado.**
2. Necesitas comprar huevos y leche **para preperar el desayuno de los niños.**
3. María y José **caminan por el Centro Comercial.**
4. María usa su tarjeta de crédito **para pagar las compras en la panadería.**
5. Esos limones **son deliciosos para preparar un pastel.**
6. ¿Les gusta el atún **o prefieren pasta para la cena?**

Now make sentences with these words.

- Tarjeta de débito
  Todas las mañanas camino a la oficina, compro mi café y pago con mi tarjeta de débito.

- Recibo
  Siempre pido los recibos cuando compro algo.

- Mercado
  Ayer compré unas fresas deliciosas en el mercado

- Cajero
  El cajero de la panadería tiene una gorra azul con el logo de la empresa.

- Fuimos
  Ayer fuimos a la verdulería y compramos lechuga, tomate, cebolla, zanahoria y apio para preparar una ensalada.

Can you answer these questions?

- ¿Dónde está la entrada del Centro Comercial?
  La entrada del Centro Comercial está a dos cuadras.

- ¿Cuál es el horario de atención durante los sábados?
  El horario de atención de los días sábado es de 10 a 22 hs.

- ¿Se puede ir los domingos?
  No, el Centro Comercial está cerrado los domingos y feriados

---

The following are scrambled sentences with this new vocabulary.
Put the words in order and write the complete sentences below.

- camisa. una roja comprar Quiero
  Quiero comprar una camisa roja

- usa Patricio impermeable su llueve. cuando
  Patricio usa su impermeable cuando llueve

- un verde ¿Tiene vestido 14. talla?
  ¿Tiene un vestido verde talle 14?

- aretes Compré largos. unos
  Compré unos aretes largos.

- sandalias Esas altas. muy son
  Esas sandalias altas son muy bonitas.

- los de Me baño gustan trajes flores. con
  Me gustan los trajes de baño con flores

Grammar Review

Answer these questions using the correct verb tense.

- Adónde fuiste ayer?
  Ayer fui a la tienda de ropa

- ¿Qué compraste en la tienda?
  Compre un vestido azul, una camisa rosa y un pantalón negro.

- ¿Cuántos años tienes?
  Tengo 23 años

- ¿Cuándo es tu cumpleaños?
  Mi cumpleaños es el 15 de marzo

- ¿Estudiaste español el sábado?
  Sí, estudié español el sábado

- ¿Hay una lámpara en tu dormitorio?
  No, no hay una lámpara en mi dormitorio.

- ¿Qué hiciste la semana pasada?
  La semana pasada fui a visitar a mi abuela a Canadá.

- ¿Quién es tu mejor amigo?
  Mi mejor amigo se llama Polo y es de Escocia.

- ¿Prefieres leer o mirar la televisión?
  Prefiero leer novelas de amor.

- ¿Qué comiste para el desayuno?
  Hoy comí huevos revueltos y fruta psara mi desayuno.

- ¿Cómo llegas al supermercado?
  Tienes que caminar cinco cuadras derecho por la Avenida Castex.

- ¿Cuándo terminaste el trabajo?
  Teminé mi trabajo ayer por la noche

- ¿De dónde eres?
  Yo soy de Buenos Aires

- ¿Cómo eres?
  Soy muy honesto, generoso y sincero.

- ¿Fuiste al parque esta semana?
  Sí, esta semana fui 3 veces a coorer por el parque

Preposition Review

More than one option is correct in many sentences. (Example answers)

- Tengo un lápiz **para** rosa.
- Los libros están **encima** de la mesa.
- Yo pago por los productos del supermercado **con** tarjeta de crédito.
- La niña está **entre** tú y yo.
- Nosotros estudiamos **cerca de** una hora.
- Los zapatos están **debajo** de la mesa.
- Ella juega **con** su amiga.
- María habla **sobre** historia en la clase de español.
- Mi cocina está **cerca de** la sala.
- Pablo puso las bolsas **sobre** la mesa.

Chapter 18

Write más or menos and que according to your opinion.

María y Julia son	más	bonitas	que	Daniela y Eva
El té y el café son	más	saludables	que	el vino y el whisky
El león está	menos	hambriento	que	el caballo
El elefante es	Más	pesado	que	el ratón
La luna está	menos	cerca	que	el sol
El avión vuela	Más	alto	que	el helicóptero
La música clásica es	Más	agradable	que	el rock
Estas patatas están	menos	saladas	que	la pizza

Write your own comparisons. (Example answers) Using the following nouns, adjectives, and verbs. You will need to modify the adjective according to the subject you choose. For example: Ella es más simpática que tu prima Estela.

Yo	somos	simpático	yo
Tus amigos	soy	inteligente	tus amigos
Los niños	es	atlético	los niños
Ella	son	gracioso	ella
El Sr. Perez		trabajador	el Sr. Perez
Nosotras		ordenado	nosotras
Mis amigos y yo		activo	mis amigos y yo
Mi primo Carlos		tímido	tu prima Estela

- **Yo soy más trabajadora que ella.**
- **Ella es más ordenada que tus amigos.**
- **Nosotras somos más activas que tu prima Estela.**
- **Mis amigos y yo somos más simpáticos que el Sr Perez.**
- **Mi primo Carlos es más gracioso que yo.**
- **El Sr Perez es más tímido que yo.**
- **Los niños son más activos que nosotras.**

Complete the following sentences using irregular comparative adjectives.

- Estas manzanas parecen **mejores** que aquellos plátanos verdes.
- Carolina cocina **peor** que su mamá.
- Las hamburguesas son **peores** que la comida de mi casa.
- Esas niñas son **menores** que mis vecinas.
- Mi esposo es **menor** que mi padre.
- Esta mesa está **mejor** que las sillas.

Comparing equality nouns

Look at the rest of the sentence to find the other half of the pair before deciding which one to put in the blank.

a. Mis amigos son tan jóvenes **como** mis primos.
b. Yo soy más débil **que** tú.
c. Nosotros somos menos fuertes **que** ellos.
d. Mi silla es tan roja **como** tu silla.
e. Mi hermana corre más rápido **que** Andrea.
f. El camión va más despacio **que** el tren.
g. Mi almuerzo no es tan abundante **como** el desayuno de Felipe.
h. La sandía no es tan dulce **como** el melón.
i. El Centro Comercial es más pequeño **que** el parque.
j. El Museo es menos popular **que** el Centro Comercial.

Comparison Practice

Read aloud these sentences. Underline the comparative or superlative phrases.

Ella es **más rápida que** su maestro.
Las sillas de la sala son **mejores que** las sillas de la cocina.
La manzana es **la mejor** fruta.
Briana es **la más inteligente** de su clase.
Los tenedores están **más limpios que** las cucharas.
Marcos es **tan estudioso como** su amigo.
Mi hermano es **tan perezoso como** yo.
Las lámparas son **menos viejas que** las sábanas.
El comedor es **más grande que** la cocina.
El desayuno es **mejor que** el almuerzo.

Read about this person's home. After reading write some sentences about your home that compare it to this home. There are a few questions underneath the paragraph to get you started.

Yo vivo en una casa. No es una casa grande, pero es muy luminosa.
Solo tiene un piso. En mi casa hay un baño, un dormitorio y una cocina.
No tiene una sala. Tiene un comedor muy grande. En mi dormitorio,
tengo una cama y un escritorio. Yo trabajo en el escritorio. En la cocina,
hay dos sillas y una mesa pequeña. Mis dos tenedores, dos cucharas
y tres cuchillos están en la cocina. En el baño tengo una toalla.

You can answer these questions or start your paragraph about what is different or similar.

- ¿Cuántas toallas tienes?
- ¿Tu casa es más grande o más pequeña?
- ¿El comedor de tu casa es tan pequeño?
- ¿Tienes más muebles en tu dormitorio?
- ¿Es más o menos luminosa?

(Example answers)

Yo no vivo en una casa. Vivo en un apartamento. Es un espacio muy grande, no tan grande como tu casa. Tampoco es tan luminoso. Es un poco oscuro porque hay muchos edificios alrededor. Mi apartamento tiene tres dormitorios y dos baños, una cocina con un espacio para almorzar o cenar y una sala tan grande que podemos recibir muchos amigos. Tenemos más sillones que sillas. No tenemos un comedor formal asi que nos reunimos en la sala cuando recibimos visitas. Mi dormitorio es el que tiene más muebles. Los demás tienen menos. Yo trabajo desde la cocina. Me gusta estar cerca de la máquina de café y soy el que toma más café de mi familia. Los baños del apartamento son muy amplios y podemos guardar las toallas junto con las sábanas y las frazadas en un armario especial. Es un apartamento muy cómodo para todos. Está muy bien ubicado, cerca de las paradas de ómnibus y el barrio tiene muchos negocios.

Comparison Review

Complete the missing words and complete this paragraph to describe one person. The options for the blanks are- *quince, más, menos, tan, amigo, escuela, guapo, música.*

Yo tengo un **amigo**. Se llama Marcos. Marcos es **tan** alto que yo. Marcos tiene pelo rubio y tiene **quince** años. Marcos es atlético. Yo también soy atlético. Marcos es **tan** atlético como yo. A Marcos le gusta dibujar. A mí no me gusta dibujar. Yo soy **menos** artístico que Marcos. Nos gusta escuchar **música** juntos. Vamos a la misma **escuela**. Después de clase, vamos a comer. Marcos come mucha comida. Yo no como tanto. Marcos paga la comida. Marcos es el estudiante más **guapo** de toda la escuela.

Chapter 19

As a warmup practice, complete the correct tense and form of the following points:

- Yo/estar/ present — **estoy**
- Ellos/estar/ preterite — **estuvieron**
- Nosotros/estar/ present — **estamos**
- Tú/estar/ present — **estás**
- Él/ estar/ preterite — **está**
- Ella/ estar/ present — **está**

Write the gerund of these verbs in parenthesis in order to build correct sentences:

- Estamos **jugando** (jugar) tenis en el parque.
- Carolina está **cantando** (cantar) con Rafael.
- Martín y yo estamos **mirando** (mirar) una película de suspenso.
- Mi mamá está **cocinando** (cocinar) un pastel de manzanas.
- Federico está **caminando** (caminar) por el Centro Comercial.
- Nosotros estamos **subiendo** (subir) las escaleras.
- Tomás está **bailando** (bailar) tango con Mercedes.
- Mariano y Enrique están **hablando** (hablar) sobre sus viajes.
- Mis vecinos están **reparando** (reparar) la puerta de su casa ahora.
- Andrés está **escribiendo** (escribir) una novela romántica.
- Yo estoy **trabajando** (trabajar) con Esteban en el proyecto.

Write the negative sentence of the following ones:

- María está manejando ahora.
- **María no está manejando ahora.**
- Juana estudia todos los días.
- **Juana no estudia todos los días**
- Tú y tus amigos juegan fútbol en el parque.
- **Tú y tus amigos no juegan fútbol en el parque.**
- Martín trabaja mucho en su computadora.
- **Martín no trabaja mucho en su computadora.**
- Nosotros estamos hablando sobre la fiesta de ayer.
- **Nosotros no estamos hablando sobre la fiesta de ayer.**
- Yo hablo inglés.
- **Yo no hablo inglés.**
- Nosotros cantamos mucho.
- **Nosotros no cantamos mucho.**
- Mis amigos están escribiendo en sus cuadernos.
- **Mis amigos no están escribiendo en sus cuadernos.**
- El gato está haciendo mucho ruido.
- **El gato no está haciendo mucho ruido.**
- Tú estás leyendo un libro de aventuras.
- **Tú no estás leyendo un libro de aventuras.**

Chapter 20

Turn each of the following sentences in present tense into future tense.

• Yo bebo	**Yo beberé**
• Ellos venden	**Ellos venderán**
• Nosotros hablamos	**Nosotros hablaremos**
• Tú descansas	**Tú descansarás**
• Él comparte	**Él compartirá**
• Mis padres abren	**Mis padres abrirán**
• Usted monta	**Usted montará**
• Vosotros limpiáis	**Vosotros limpiareis**
• Yo corro	**Yo correré**
• Nosotros enseñamos	**Nosotros enseñaremos**

Fill in the blanks with the correctly conjugated *ir* for each of the following sentences.

1. Nosotros **vamos** a practicar fútbol.
2. Ellos **van** a tratar de aprender el español.
3. Yo **voy** a cambiar las luces.
4. Ella **va** a llamar a su amigo.
5. Tú **vas** a jugar tenis con Marcela.
6. Usted **va** a trabajar mañana.
7. Ustedes **van** a cantar en la fiesta.
8. Yo **voy** a saltar mucho.
9. Ellas **van** a jugar a las cartas.
10. Nosotras **vamos** a hacer compras.

Read the following conversation out loud.
Then, answer the questions below. (Example answers)

Antonio: ¿Qué vas a hacer este fin de semana?
José: Yo voy a estudiar mucho. Tengo un examen el lunes.
Antonio: ¿Para qué clase es tu examen?
José: Es para español. Quiero salir con mis amigos, pero me quedaré estudiando.
Antonio: Yo voy a la casa de mis abuelos. Mis abuelos me llevarán al Restaurante La Parolaccia.
José: Mmmm, ¡que rico!

1. ¿Qué hará José este fin de semana?
José estudiará mucho.

2. ¿Por qué va a estudiar?
Estudiará porque tiene un examen el lunes.

3. ¿A qué restaurante irá Antonio?
Antonio irá a La Parolaccia.

Read aloud this conversation and answer the questions.

Juan: Hoy es el último día de escuela. ¿Qué harás durante las vacaciones de verano?
Tomás: No sé. Quiero ir a la playa, pero mis hermanos quieren ir a las montañas. Creo que iremos a acampar.
Juan: ¿Te gusta acampar?
Tomás: No mucho. Yo prefiero leer un libro o escuchar música en la playa. ¿Qué planes tienes tú?
Juan: Yo voy a volar a Italia y pasaré junio allá. Luego, voy a Canadá por un mes. Dibujaré mucho y no tendré que hacer nada de libros ni estudios.
Tomás: ¡Suena bien divertido!
Juan: ¿Vas a venir conmigo?
Tomás: Quiero, pero no puedo.

1. ¿Adónde va Juan en sus vacaciones?
Juan irá a acampar.

2. ¿En qué se diferencia Tomás de sus hermanos?
El quiere ir a la playa y sus hermanos, no. Además, prefiere leer libros o escuchar música.

3. ¿Qué quiere hacer Tomás?
Quiere ir con Juan, pero no puede.

In this practice, you must fill in the blank with the verb in the correct future tense. Sometimes, you will need to use the "will" future form, and others need to use the "going" future form.

1. Mario y yo **haremos** un pastel para el cumpleaños de mi mamá.
2. Beatriz **va** a **trabajar** en una oficina nueva.
3. Martina, ¿**vas** a ir a la fiesta mañana?
4. Mis amigos **van** a ganar mil dólares.
5. Manolo **recordará** todo del horario.
6. Manuel y Carlos **vamos** a nadar en la laguna.
7. Victoria y Teresa **visitarán** a sus padres el mes que viene
8. Marcelo **va** a comprar papas y hamburguesas.
9. Camilo, ¿**comerás** esa porción de pizza?
10. Yo **volaré** en helicóptero por la ciudad de Nueva York.
11. Tú **correrás** una maratón de 10 millas.
12. Miranda va a comprar un libro de cuentos infantil.
13. Nosotras **vamos** a limpiar la casa mañana.
14. Nosotras no **vamos** de vacaciones en febrero.
15. No **voy** a trabajar el próximo sábado.

Let's do one more practice!
Read the sentence in one form of the future tense and change it to the other.

1. Ellos estudiarán por tres horas.	**Ellos van a estudiar por tres horas.**
2. Nosotros diremos la verdad.	**Ellos van a decir la verdad.**
3. Yo me dormiré muy tarde.	**Yo me voy a dormir muy tarde.**
4. Tú llevarás un vestido bonito.	**Tú vas a llevar un vestido muy bonito.**
5. Bárbara va a estudiar.	**Bárbara estudiará.**
6. Mis amigos van a llamar a la maestra.	**Mis amigos llamarán a la maestra.**
7. Tú no vas a esperar mucho tiempo.	**Tú no esperarás mucho tiempo.**

Chapter 21

Which tense is it?

Identify the tense of the following verbs. Remember their meaning and the subject pronoun (yo, tú, él, ella, usted, nosotros, ellos, ustedes) as well.

1. Estoy trabajando.
2. Yo bebo.
3. Ellas practican.
4. Ellos practicaron.
5. Camila va a estudiar.
6. Yo no trabajé.
7. Nosotros enseñamos.
8. Miguel habló.
9. Yo no montaré ese caballo.
10. Tú no estás limpiando.

Fill in the blanks

Choose one of the following verbs off the list to complete the following paragraphs. First, read the verbs and find each meaning. Then read the paragraph to discover which verb is missing in each blank. Select the verb that makes sense for each sentence and change the ending to the correct tense.

Using the past tense: vivir, asignar, ser, hablar, vender, llevar, trabajar

Hace tres años, yo viví en una casa grande. Había tres dormitorios, pero el sofá de la sala era siempre mi lugar preferido para descansar. Una mañana, mi carro se descompuso, entonces un amigo vino a casa y me llevó al trabajo. Llegué muy tarde y mi jefe (boss) me asignó muchas tareas. No me gustó trabajar tanto. Después de un año, yo vendí la casa y me mudé a un apartamento.

Using the two options to conjugate a verb in the future tense: volver, cambiar, hacer, vivir, esperar, llamar, dormir, jugar, ir

Example option 1:

Después de la escuela, yo iré a la universidad. Viviré en mi nuevo apartamento desde agosto y esperaré hasta que empiecen las clases. Yo haré muchos amigos y nosotros jugaremos fútbol después de clase. Mi mamá me llamará muchas veces para hablar conmigo. Yo me dormiré muy tarde en la noche y tú cambiarás tu horario para tener clases conmigo.

Example option 2:

Después de la escuela, yo voy a ir a la universidad. Voy a vivir en mi nuevo apartamento desde agosto y voy a esperar hasta que empiecen las clases. Yo voy a hacer muchos amigos y nosotros vamos a jugar fútbol después de clase. Mi mamá me va a llamar muchas veces para hablar conmigo. Yo me voy a dormir muy tarde en la noche y tú vas a cambiarás tu horario para tener clases conmigo.

Write your own sentences

Write your own sentences with each of the following words. After the space, a sample sentence has been provided. (Example sentences)

Voy / **Yo voy a limpiar la casa todos los días.**
Yo voy a escribir una carta a mi madre.

Sin / **Sin luz, no podemos trabajar.**
No quiero comer sin agua.

También / **También compré huevos para comer un pastel.**
Ellos también quieren venir.

Dos / **Dos gatos caminan por la calle sin temores.**
Hay dos puertas en mi salón de clase.

Estás / **Tú estás trabajando mucho.**
Tú estás manejando muy rápido.

Menos / **Tres menos uno es dos.**
Yo soy menos inteligente que él.

Entre / **El niño entá entre su mamá y su papá**
Mi ordenador está entre las lámparas.

Debajo de / **El ratón está debajo de la heladera.**
Yo busco mi lápiz debajo del sofá.

Fueron / **Los jugadores fueron al partido con mucha decisión.**
Mis amigos fueron a la escuela a las nueve y media.

Izquierda / **No puedo escribir con mi mano izquierda.**
La gasolinera está a la izquierda de la biblioteca.

Now, write some questions using the following words.
Once again, sample questions have been provided for you.

¿Qué? **¿Qué quieres hacer para cenar?**
¿Qué estás haciendo?

¿Dónde? **¿Dónde puedo encontrar un hospital?**
¿Dónde está tu casa?

¿Quién? **¿Quién es el Presidente de los Estados Unidos?**
¿Quién es tu mejor amigo?

¿Cuál? **¿Cuál es tu película favorita?**
¿Cuál es tu comida favorita?

¿Cuándo? **¿Cuándo vamos a la oficina?**
¿Cuándo es tu clase de español?

Reading practice
Story 1 (Example answers).

1. ¿Cuántas mascotas tiene Gabriela?
- **Gabriela tiene cinco mascotas.**

2. ¿Cuáles son las mascotas?
- **Las mascotas son dos perros, dos tortugas y un gato.**

3. ¿Cómo son los perros?
- **Un perro es blanco con manchas negras y el otro es gris.**

4. ¿Qué animal recibirá Gabriela?
- **Gabriela recibirá una tortuga.**

Story 2 /example answers).

Go ahead and read this second story which follows more of a typical story pattern.
Once again, identify the verbs and find their meanings before answering questions.

Pablo estudió mucho para su examen de inglés durante todo el día. Su madre entró en su dormitorio.
—Pablo, ¿qué haces? —le preguntó su madre.
—Estudio, Mamá. Necesito aprobar el examen.
—Bueno, la cena está lista. Puedes comer con nosotros.
Pablo bajó por las escaleras hacia la cocina y comió una cena deliciosa. Su mamá hizo puré de papas y pollo, la cena favorita de Pablo.
—Gracias, mamá. Está muy rico.
-Ahora, vas a estudiar otra vez.
Pablo llevó su libro a la sala y estudió allí. Leyó un largo rato hasta que su hermana entró y le habló.
—Pablo, ¿qué haces?
—¡Estudio! —gritó Pablo.
—Quiero jugar contigo.
—No, no puedo jugar. Estudiaré en mi dormitorio —dijo Pablo y regresó a su dormitorio otra vez.

What verbs did you find?
Complete the table with ten verbs of the dialogue and their tenses.

	Verb	Tense
1	Estudió	Past tense
2	Entró	Past tense
3	Preguntó	Past tense
4	Necesito	Past tense
5	Está	Present tense
6	Bajó	Past tense
7	Hizo	Past tense
8	Llevó	Past tense
9	Leyó	Past tense
10	Habló	Past tense

Now, answer these questions.

1. ¿Qué hace Pablo?
Pablo estudia.

2. ¿Dónde estudia?
Estudia en su dormitorio

3. ¿Por qué estudia?
Estudia porque necesita aprobar un examen.

4. ¿Qué comió Pablo?
Pablo comió puré de papas y pollo.

These are the basic body parts.
Before we add in some phrases let's practice! Find these words.

NARIZ	BOCA	LENGUA	OREJA	PELO	NUCA	OMBLIGO
HOMBRO	ESPALDA	TORSO	FRENTE	MEJILLA	PIERNA	CODO
MANO	DEDO	ESTOMAGO	NALGA	TOBILLO	DIENTE	PECHO
	CINTURA	RODILLA	VENAS	MUSCULO	LABIOS	

```
J M Y E Y F M U S C U L O X
V J I D V R Y E X O O J C Q
L T C K E E H S W D S X I Y
E B O F N N O T V O G W N O
N P D R A T M O R E J A T M
G E R I S E B M X F P A U B
U L O P E O R A N R E X R L
A O D I R N O G A Q C D A I
Y C I E T A T O R H E M G
B J L R Q L B E I R O D A O
M B L N Q G O V Z O N O N R
S Z A A E A C J O J G U O K
M E J I L L A B I O S O C G
E S P A L D A V J S P I V A
```

Read aloud the following Spanish sentences. Connect with lines their meanings

Tuve un accidente	I am sick
Tengo fiebre	I have pain in my back.
Usted necesita cirugía de rodilla	I had an accident
Estoy enfermo	You need knee surgery
Necesito atención urgente	I have allergies to peanut
Tengo una herida en mi pierna	My throat is swollen
Tengo dolor de espalda	I have a fever
Me duele el estómago	I did not drink a lot of water
No bebí mucha agua	Brush your teeth
Mi garganta está inflamada	I need urgent attention
Tengo alergias a los cacahuates	I have an injury in my leg.
Cepilla tus dientes	My stomach hurts

Let's make some sentences now. Remember to start with the person it hurts first.
(Example answers)

• Make a sentence about your nose hurting you.
Me duele mucho la nariz.

• Make a sentence about your friend's finger hurting.
A mi amigo Juan le duele mucho el dedo.

• Make a sentence about both of your arms hurting.
Me duelen mucho mis dos brazos

Practicing Medical Vocabulary
(Example answers)

1. ¿Qué parte del cuerpo le duele?
A Martín le duele la espalda.

2. ¿Cuánto tiempo hace que le duele la espalda?
A Martín le duele la espalda hace dos días.

Let's pretend that your finger hurts.
Answer the following questions that a doctor might ask you about it. (Example answers)

1. ¿Qué le duele?
Me duele el dedo, doctor

2. ¿De la mano izquierda o derecha?
Me duele el dedo de la mano derecha.

3. En una escala de uno a diez, ¿cuánto le duele?
Me duele 8.

4. ¿Tuvo un accidente?
Si, me caí en la calle.

5. ¿Usted puede mover el dedo?
No puedo moverlo mucho. Está inflamado

6. ¿Usted tomó pastillas para el dolor?
No, doctor. No tomé nada. Usé hielo.